Museums as Agents for Social Change

Museums as Agents for Social Change is the first comprehensive text to examine museum practice in a decolonised moment, moving beyond known roles of object collection and presentation.

Drawing on studies of Mutare Museum, a regional museum in Eastern Zimbabwe, this book considers how museums with inherited colonial legacies are dealing with their new environments. The book provides an examination of Mutare Museum's activism in engaging with topical issues affecting its surrounding community, and Chipangura and Mataga demonstrate how new forms of engagement are being deployed to attract new audiences, whilst dealing with issues such as economic livelihoods, poverty, displacement, climate change and education. Illustrating how recent programmes have helped to reposition Mutare Museum as a decolonial agent of social change and an important community anchor institution, the book also demonstrates how other museums can move beyond the colonial preoccupation with the gathering of collections, conservation and presentation of cultural heritage to the public.

Museums as Agents for Social Change will primarily be of interest to academics and students working in the fields of museum and heritage studies, history, archaeology and anthropology. It should also be appealing to museum professionals around the world who are interested in learning more about how to decolonise their museum.

Njabulo Chipangura is a postdoctoral research fellow at the Centre for Urbanism and Built Environment Studies (CUBES), School of Architecture and Planning, University of the Witwatersrand, Johannesburg, South Africa and a visiting fellow in the Museum and Gallery Practice Programme at University College London, Qatar. He previously worked as curator of archaeology at Mutare Museum, Eastern Zimbabwe for ten years.

Jesmael Mataga is an associate professor of Heritage Studies and head of the School of Humanities at Sol Plaatje University (SPU), a new university in Kimberley, South Africa. He previously worked for the National Museums and Monuments of Zimbabwe (NMMZ) and taught at the University of Zimbabwe and at the National University of Lesotho.

Museums in Focus
Series Editor: Kylie Message, Australian National University, Australia

Committed to the articulation of big, even risky ideas, in small format publications, '*Museums in Focus*' challenges authors and readers to experiment with, innovate, and press museums and the intellectual frameworks through which we view these. It offers a platform for approaches that radically rethink the relationships between cultural and intellectual dissent and crisis and debates about museums, politics and the broader public sphere.

'*Museums in Focus*' is motivated by the intellectual hypothesis that museums are not innately 'useful', 'safe' or even 'public' places, and that recalibrating our thinking about them might benefit from adopting a more radical and oppositional form of logic and approach. Examining this problem requires a level of comfort with (or at least tolerance of) the idea of crisis, dissent, protest and radical thinking, and authors might benefit from considering how cultural and intellectual crisis, regeneration and anxiety have been dealt with in other disciplines and contexts.

The following list includes only the most-recent titles to publish within the series. A list of the full catalogue of titles is available at: https://www.routledge.com/Museums-in-Focus/book-series/MIF

Queering the Museum
Nikki Sullivan and Craig Middleton

Museums as Agents for Social Change
Collaborative Programmes at the Mutare Museum
Njabulo Chipangura and Jesmael Mataga

Museums and Atlantic Slavery
Ana Lucia Araujo

MUSEUMS IN FOCUS

Logo by James Verdon (2017)

Museums as Agents for Social Change

Collaborative Programmes at the Mutare Museum

Njabulo Chipangura and Jesmael Mataga

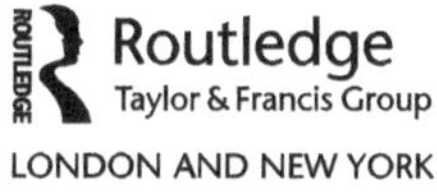

LONDON AND NEW YORK

First published 2021
by Routledge
2 Park Square, Milton Park, Abingdon, Oxon OX14 4RN

and by Routledge
605 Third Avenue, New York, NY 10158

Routledge is an imprint of the Taylor & Francis Group, an informa business

British Library Cataloguing-in-Publication Data
A catalogue record for this book is available from the British Library

Library of Congress Cataloging-in-Publication Data
A catalog record has been requested for this book

ISBN: 978-0-367-21780-8 (hbk)
ISBN: 978-1-032-01916-1 (pbk)
ISBN: 978-0-429-26604-1 (ebk)

Typeset in Times New Roman
by KnowledgeWorks Global Ltd.

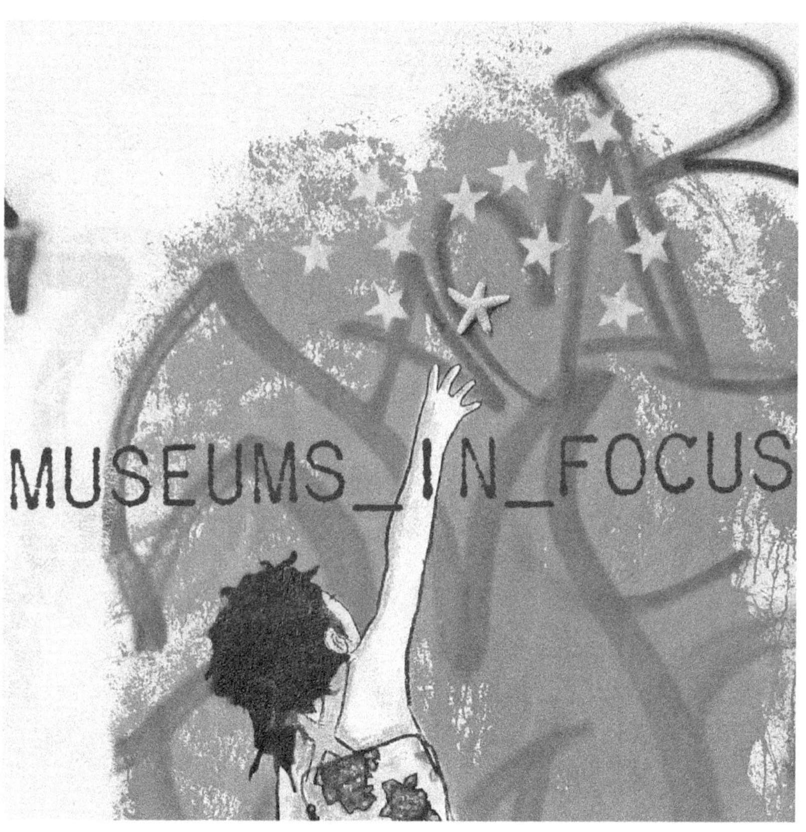

Anonymous graffiti, Athens. Image and logo by James Verdon (2017).

Contents

Figures

Preface

The question of how museums, in spite of their histories, can continually reinvent and transform themselves into sites for engagement with diverse communities, is topical, urgent and universal. The ongoing debates on changing the definition of a museum by the International Council of Museums (ICOM) encapsulate this universal desire for more inclusive engagements with communities. In Africa, where the origins of museums were intricately tied with colonial domination and conquest of the continent, the need for changing museums has been persistent. This book, beyond acknowledging the colonial origins of African museums, seeks to foreground strategies that have been used to deal with this past, while engendering a "decolonial" future for museum-community relationships in Africa. Drawing from activities of a regional museum in Eastern Zimbabwe, this book explores strategies that can be deployed by museums with inherited colonial legacies, in dealing with this past in new environments. We foreground how small museums, formed in the colonial era, managed by centralized state systems, are finding innovative ways to deal with their tainted colonial past, where the museums were formed for selected races and classes and served narrow audiences. We highlight methods, activities and forms of engagement with local communities, adopted for their transformation in the postcolonial contexts, as the museums seek to unsettle the race/class eclecticism ingrained in their past. Our case studies are drawn from activities around four programmes the Mutare Museum. The Mutare Museum is one of the five regional museums that is under the administration of National Museums and Monuments of Zimbabwe (NMMZ), a state-supported body that manages all national museums and heritage sites in Zimbabwe. The chosen activities in this book show how new forms of engagement are being deployed, using objects and spaces in the museums, as well as sites outside of the museum, to engage with marginal communities and to attract new audiences by dealing with new issues such as economic livelihood, poverty, displacement, climate change and education. Using the various archaeological sites that it manages, and a reworking of its exhibitions, the museum has initiated public programmes aimed at challenging colonial museum and heritage preservation practices while addressing social, cultural, economic and educational considerations of the society.

The attention to and writing on contemporary issues in history museums is relatively new in Zimbabwe, and in Africa and like other post-colonial nations, we are seeking inclusive initiatives that acknowledge the communities' own needs and versions of the past, using the museum as a site of engagement. By using selected examples of museum projects, this book illustrates how these programmes have repositioned Mutare Museum in its new role of being an activist museum and decolonial agent of social change. We argue that by becoming an important community anchor institution, Mutare Museum has transcended its colonial outlook whose preoccupation was underpinned by gathering of collections, conservation and presentation of cultural heritage to the public into becoming an interactive space where day-to-day challenges are discussed. More importantly, by partaking in social activities that have a bearing on communities' aspirations, Mutare Museum has managed to offset authorised colonial discursive practices which were largely based on collecting ethnographic objects for the scientific gaze. Most communities in Zimbabwe have regarded the museum as an elitist urban institution where local communities felt marginalised and aggrieved by the fact that ethnographic objects appropriated from them were displayed in the museum devoid of their social context and meaning. However, the case of Mutare Museum shows how such small museums can engage differently with their local stakeholders by creating spaces (within and without the museum) where critical dialogue on contemporary challenges are discussed, invoked, promoted and sometimes challenged. In line with their new vision of social activism, museums can transform themselves into multivocal spaces for dialogue in curating both objects and stories.

This book contributes to the ongoing global debates on decolonizing the museum practice by using empirical examples drawn from Mutare Museum, arguing that in spite of its history, the museum still occupies a central role in how communities engage and imagine the present and deal with social change. We show that by drawing on its objects, identified social concerns (such as effects of mining on local communities), and by working through sites outside of the museum to address social issues, the institution has transcended its inherited legacies, repositioning the museum in a new role as an agent of social change. This paradigm shift not only reconfigured the colonial frame of this museum but also brought with it multivocal museological practices which increased its relevancy through public engagement, participation and representation. Theoretically, the book draws on the notions of decoloniality to highlight the need for museums to critically engage with their colonial pasts. While acknowledging the ambivalent nature of the debates around the notion of decolonisation, for this book, decolonisation entails strategies by which earlier forms of knowledge production which were structured by colonial classificatory categories were challenged through community collaborations, not only did the initiatives that were embraced bring about epistemological change – there has also been an ontological re-orientation around how the local communities regard their objects as living beings connected to their everyday lives. While for a long time, most communities in Zimbabwe regarded the museum as an elitist urban space that propagated ideas of social exclusion, case studies in *Museums, Decolonisation and Social Change: Collaborative Programmes* at the Mutare Museum will also show how Mutare Museum has adopted strategies that positively impacted on the lives of disadvantaged and marginalised individuals while at the same time acting as a catalyst for social change. Such practices at the museum were informed by deliberate strategies that involved communities in collaborative decision making and inclusive resource governance structures.

Acknowledgments

Projects on research and writing are usually credited to a few, yet the processes and the end products are always a result of intricate relationships, varied inputs from different stakeholders and thus a communal effort. Our sincere appreciation goes to the local communities who live around most of the sites discussed in this volume, and who have taken an opportunity to insert themselves back into the museum and engage in the various activities described in this text. This ranges from the local traditional, political and religious leaders to ordinary members of society. In taking part in these activities and allowing us to understand and analyse them, these communities have profoundly contributed to knowledge production. These views and experiences from Africa are crucial in reshaping the universal discourses and debates about the ever-changing role of museums in society.

The authors extend appreciation to the various organisations, communities and people who played an important role in the making of this book. We acknowledge the resources provided by the NMMZ and Mutare Museum. We also acknowledge the following institutions:

UCL Qatar for awarding Dr Njabulo Chipangura a visiting fellowship to write some chapters of this book; the Centre for Urbanism and Built Environment Studies (CUBES), University of the Witwatersrand, Johannesburg, where Dr Chipangura is currently based; and Sol Plaatje University for the financial support to Prof J. Mataga for a research visit to Zimbabwe.

Our sincere appreciation goes to the Routledge editorial team, especially Heidi Lowther.

Introduction

Museum pasts and decolonised futures in Africa

The question of how to define a museum has been a festering debate globally, and particularly for previously colonized societies who inherited the institution from a specific historical period – the colonial era, which fostered oppression, marginalisation and ostracisation of colonised societies. In the post-colonial context, beyond contests over the definition of museums, the major debates and discussions have been on the role and relevance of museums within the wider society. Thus, as the museum world rethinks the current definition, it is perhaps also a good moment to critically reflect on how museums do create spaces for effectively dealing with societies and remaining relevant. For many museums in Africa created during colonial subjugation, museum knowledge production, classification and representation practices structured ethnographic collections in accordance with Western epistemological thoughts. For many such institutions, this is the moment to address the intellectual and emotional processes of decolonisation in terms of repatriation of objects or developing collaborative projects with communities (Sandahl 2019). This book draws on the ongoing debates around the coloniality of museums and associated knowledge production and representation practices to imagine a decolonised museum in Africa. In this Introduction, we set the background and context of these debates, as well as the historical and current contexts of museums in Zimbabwe, before providing a specific narrative on the development of Mutare Museum in Eastern Zimbabwe. We argue that the decolonial future of museums lies in them challenging their histories and normative practices by a mingling with heritage sites, local cultural practices and ways of knowing. To demonstrate this, this book moves between the museum, selected sites and associated practices.

(Re)defining museums: towards a decolonised approach

At the time of writing this book, a new museum definition was proposed and debated at the International Council of Museums (ICOM) General Conference in Kyoto, Japan in September 2019. The first author, Njabulo Chipangura, was privileged to attend this meeting as a young museum grantee courtesy of a generous grant from the Getty Foundation. In the heated debates on what should constitute the best definition of a museum there was no agreement, and as a result voting for the new definition was postponed indefinitely. ICOM had proposed changing the museum definition in order to embrace alternative world views, cosmologies and epistemologies that recognizes the connection between objects and their social points of origin, which in many ways is reflective of how decoloniality in museum practice can be articulated (Sandahl 2019).

The current shared definition currently used views a museum as "a non-profit, permanent institution in the service of society and its development that is open to the public and acquires, conserves, researches, communicates and exhibits tangible and intangible heritage of humanity and its environment for the purposes of education, study and enjoyment" (ICOM 2017). For a section of the global museum community, this definition has not changed for almost fifty years and has become outdated as reflected by its failure to articulate on rapid change and prospects and future potentials of museums (Sandahl 2019). The proposed 2019 definition characterized museums as:

> democratizing, inclusive and polyphonic spaces for critical dialogue about the pasts and the futures. Acknowledging and addressing the conflicts and challenges of the present, they hold artefacts and specimens in trust for society, safeguard diverse memories for future generations and guarantee equal rights and equal access to heritage for all people. They are participatory and transparent, and work in active partnership with and for diverse communities to collect, preserve, research, interpret, exhibit, and enhance understandings of the world, aiming to contribute to human dignity and social justice, global equality and planetary wellbeing. (ICOM,2019: 3)

Whilst in the past the museum and its core function of collecting and exhibiting objects was separated from social responsibilities, for those advocating for the new definition, this proposed characterization integrates all these aspects. Most importantly, as argued by Sandahl

(2019: 2) and as we are also going to demonstrate, "... the definition ... express the unity of the role of museums with the collaboration and shared commitment, responsibility and authority in relation to their communities." For us in this book, an inclusive definition should look at a museum as a space for tangible or intangible heritage that provides an opportunity for transfer of knowledge and is open to the public (Ariese-Vandemeulebroucke 2018: 39). This is because a decolonial perspective in museum practice acknowledges that objects are not mundane but rather represent the coming together of a multiplicity of factors (Chipangura and Chipangura 2020). Such an approach puts reconnection with society as a central tenet of the future function of museums. This is particularly important for Africa, where museums were introduced as part of subjugation of local economies, cultures and political entities during the colonial era. The museum, which developed as a handmaiden of colonialism, has a duty to rid itself of its history as it adjusts to new social realities in contemporary Africa.

However, it is important to acknowledge the fact that this new proposed definition was fraught with contestation, disagreements and divergent reactions amongst delegates at the 2019 ICOM General Conference. In the General Conference's discussions, the definition was critiqued by representatives mostly from European countries as a prescriptive ideological manifesto with political undertones that ignored the traditional function of a museum. The other critique was that the new definition seemed to be reducing the museum into a social mixed bag for everything and thus negating its fundamental core functions. Fraser (2019: 503), writing about the new definition, argues that "...it also seemed that there was a rush to gather all of the world's contemporary problems into one large bucket and claim that museums can solve these issues." Some delegates argued that museums were increasingly getting muddled in trying to be all things to all people, and this was creating an identity crisis for them. Whilst acknowledging the divergent views on how museums should be defined and understood, we argue that for the African museum practice, the proposed definition was appropriate as it imagined the possibility of centring the social role of museums, thereby enabling the possibility of allowing African museums to re-engage with their colonial past which narrowed this function in very specific ways. The proposed new definition creates space that could bring together many of the decolonial initiatives and strategies that we share in this book. From our point of view, the new definition calls for greater acknowledgement of the history of colonialism in many museums' collecting practices – an aspect that the museum fraternity had been grappling with for the past decade and continues to do. We argue that museums cannot avoid critically thinking about how to disengage from and reflect beyond Western epistemologies and binaries entrenched with museum practice around the world. Yet, the contested ideal of a socially inclusive museum relates well with African museum practices that are undergirded by community collaboration, inclusivity, critical dialogue and multivocality.

To give a historical context to these efforts, the book traces the formation of the Mutare Museum as a colonial creation before moving on to demonstrate how in the post-colonial period, collaborative programmes in exhibition development and sustainable heritage practices were used in creating new forms of engagement with communities. We see these strategies as contributing to the museum's transformation and to entrenchment of a process of decolonising its own inherited practices. The book argues that by collaborating with the local community, the museum also became a "contact zone" in the sense of James Clifford's 1997 concept of "contact zone" where museums have increasingly been promoting their postcolonial status through inclusionist programs in exhibitions, shared curatorship and use of collections (Pratt 1992; Clifford 2007). While the notion of contact zones has been criticized for failing to acknowledge and critique the asymmetric power relations in these engagements, there is an undeniable unprecedented improvement in the empowerment of source communities in the management, use and presentation of their patrimony in museums (Boast 2011: x). This is achieved by presenting Mutare Museum in Eastern Zimbabwe as a contact zone rooted in a plurality of world views and systems of knowledge rather than in single colonially informed Western narratives. Since this museum is inclusive in nature, we posit that it is a contact zone (Pratt 1992; Clifford 2007) that has evolved beyond the easily definable arena of conservation and presentation of objects into a space for dialogue and intercultural exchange that brings together communities and establishes ongoing collaborative relations. It is such strategies that have started the museum on a decolonising trajectory – one that provides a pathway beyond the limitations of colonial museums by using specific local ideas (McCarthy 2019). This book highlights how a museum born off a colonial process can acknowledge and live with this past, while at the same time embrace new forms of engagement. For this museum, the strategy has been new collaborative projects which are giving priority to social aspects that affect local communities as well as providing a meeting place where cultural identities of communities are revitalized (Laely, Meyer and Schwere 2018; Macdonald and Morgan 2019; Thomas 2019).

In this book we will illuminate how the Mutare Museum is advancing advocacy roles through collaborative social programmes that are effecting change (Janes and Sandell 2019). Though some in the museum world have made claims of the institutions being objective and politically neutral, in the African context this assertion cannot hold sway. This is mainly because museums in Africa are products and projects of colonialism. They were intricately embedded in the processes of colonial subjugation, and in the post-colonial era it may still be hugely misleading to think of them as being neutral and apolitical. For many, those histories mean that museums are a place where visitors should think critically about the past and the future, echoing elements of the proposed alternative definition. Museums are always political and thus we argue that decoloniality at Mutare Museum is signified through a praxis of engaging with communities where they were previously marginalised by colonial matrixes of power which "othered" their cultures. Decolonisation then also entails democratising decision making and acknowledging that museums are not neutral and have played a role in misrepresenting African cultures for a long time (Wajid and Minott 2019). Mutare Museum falls under the administration of National Museums and Monuments of Zimbabwe (NMMZ), the state-supported statutory board that manages all state museums in the country. Over the last decade the museum has initiated public programmes aimed at addressing social, cultural, economic and educational considerations of its local society and addressing contemporary issues, an aspect that in history museums is something relatively new in Zimbabwe.

Methodologically, we used a reflective approach drawn from both our positions as former employees of the NMMZ. Furthermore, in positioning the various collaborative initiatives that we engaged with as decolonial methodologies, we allowed the community voices to come to the fore. The modes of participation included individual and group discussions of personal experiences, interviews, surveys and analysis of public documents. In this regard, communities were given space to articulate their narratives and experiences in relation to museum programmes, allowing for co-construction and co-production of knowledge. As researchers, during the process of data collection, analysis and our own writing, we maintained a deliberate awareness of the interconnectivity between and among ourselves, the participants from the local communities we worked with, the data and the methods we used to interpret and analyse (Gentles and Jack 2014). We drew on our positionality as former employees and museum professionals of an organisation (NMMZ) that managed the sites that we discuss throughout the book. The first author, Njabulo Chipangura worked as a curator of archaeology at Mutare Museum from 2009 to 2020, whereas the second author was a senior curator of ethnography at the Zimbabwe Museum of Human Sciences from 1999 to 2003. Significantly, this professional experience allowed us access to internal systems, procedures and convenience in identifying and working with local communities while at the same time also allowing us to critically reflect on our own practices and those of the museum for which we had worked. In regard to our study sites, we were thus both insiders and outsiders by the fact that most of the research was completed when neither of us were still working for the organisation. This positionality, while allowing us a much closer and deeper immersion into our research sites, also required us to maintain an awareness of possible unconscious biases in our interactions with the museum, the sites we were looking at, our interactions with communities and our analysis.

As former employees of the NMMZ, we were constantly conscious of our positionality and the potential subjectivities. To mitigate this, a central aspect of our approach was to flag the voices of local communities. In our engagements we had interviews, formal and informal conversations with local traditional leaders, spiritual leaders, local political structures and community members. Our choices of who we had conversations with or observed were largely influenced by the nature and processes of the projects and programmes which we were seeking to analyse and critique. Our participants were made aware of their roles and positions, not only as sources of data, but as co-producers whose voices would be foregrounded in the narrative to emerge from the engagements. Thus, we deliberately sought to establish relationships that attempted to unsettle implied skewed power dynamics between ourselves as researchers and the community. Our forms of engagement emphasised the agency of our collaborators, and this entailed flexibility around language, dynamics of listening, acknowledgement and respect. These qualitative data were triangulated with primary written data from the Mutare Museum. We read though the museum's strategy documents, programme proposals and reports pertaining to the specific projects and programmes discussed throughout this book. We also moved between the museum, looking at programmes, curatorial exhibits and performances, and the sites in the field, where we observed, engaged with and talked to local communities. In our analysis, rather than seeking descriptive analysis of the projects and programmes at the sites, we sought to cast a critical lens, analysing, critiquing, commenting and foregrounding key themes, issues and contests.

In this book, we also acknowledge the fact that one cannot decolonise a museum without delinking its colonial matrix of power, since the practice of collecting and classifying objects is deeply embedded in colonialism itself which created the museum institution as we know it today (Abungu 2019; Vawda 2019). In this book, we will present a decolonised museum practice, which is collaborative, dialogical and sympathetic to different perspectives as it provides a framework for discussion and knowledge production through co-curation of exhibitions (Vawda 2019: 78). By extension, we will also show the enactment of decoloniality at Mutare Museum as a standpoint, analytic practice and a praxis that is located in community collaborations. This we relate to what Message (2018) defines and characterises as the "disobedient museum" – one which prioritises engagement with formerly ostracized communities outside the dictates of instrumentalised forms of knowledge production informed by scientific studies in disciplines such as archaeology, anthropology and ethnography. The "disobedient museum" is thus a typical model on which Mutare Museum is anchored as it embraces collaborations with the communities in a non-disciplinary or undisciplined way (Message 2018). In our own experience, this disobedience manifests in how a small museum in a former British colony seeks to transcend its colonial legacies by moving beyond outmoded ways of object collecting, conserving and presentation into a dialogical platform of community engagement. This disobedient approach as both a concept and a methodology essentially rethinks the various ways in which this museum engages with the contemporary social/political issues in the environment in which it is located. Traditionally, museum practice here was informed by instrumentalised forms of knowledge production supported by disciplines such as archaeology, anthropology and ethnography – always approached from a fossilized binary where the disciplinary experts treated objects and knowledge production as the ends. Converse to this, the disobedient museum is a form of engagement outside the scientific categories of knowledge production which prioritises community participation (Message 2018). While the disciplinary demarcations are respected, they are disrupted by preference for fluid movements across the disciplines. The expert, curator or scientist is no longer the sole purveyor of knowledge. Rather, the authority is shared; deliberate empowerment through recognition, community collaboration and political agency are all various strategies that are being embraced in order to decolonize the museum practice (Message 2018). Accepting communities as experts and research partners has changed the museum practice by opening up different ways of knowing and

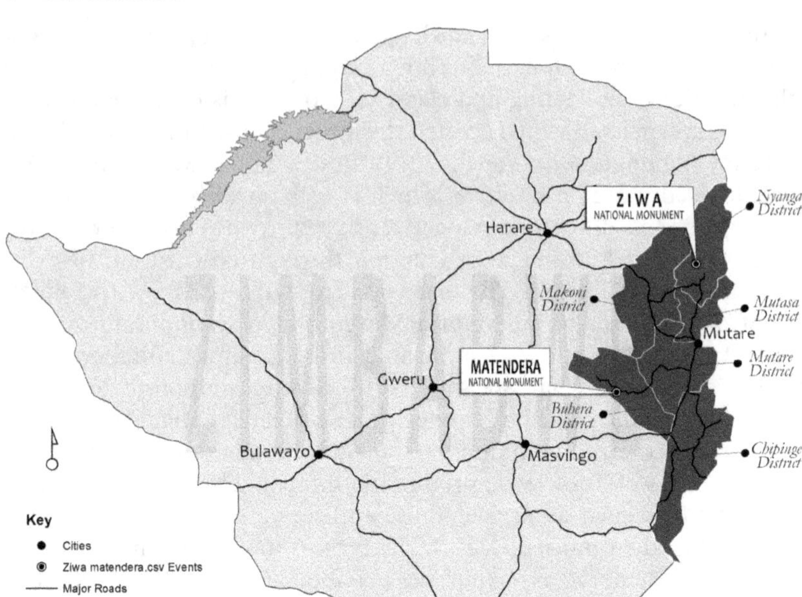

Figure 0.1 The location of Mutare Museum relative to the heritage sites where collaborative projects were undertaken. Map by Njabulo Chipangura.

caring for the past (Onciul 2019). In light of such developments, we will show how the Mutare Museum developed strategies, multidisciplinary holistic approaches and methods for interpreting objects and collections in an interrelated connection with community aspirations and ways of seeing. Whereas previously the focus of this museum was on collections and objects, we will demonstrate a fundamental shift towards societal roles that embraced activist and participatory methodologies (Figure 0.1).

Museums and local communities: Shift in Africa

What is happening at Mutare Museum has much wider implications for museum development elsewhere on the continent. Mutare is but a microcosm of the wider shared histories, developments and trajectories of museum development in colonial and postcolonial Africa. Therefore, while acknowledging the contexts within which museums were formed during the colonial period in Southern Africa, this book looks beyond this tainted history to highlight how museums have emerged in the postcolonial context, challenging processes of confinement, classification and nomenclature entrenched by colonial museum practices. It shows how museums in postcolonial Africa have the potential to play new roles in the public sphere, allowing communities previously excluded from the museum space to enter and influence curatorial activities. Through selected curatorial and community-based projects at Mutare Museum, the chapter highlights how these activities inspire a new approach to museum practice – one that has enabled a new trajectory in expert-community relations and engendered a new curatorial approach. The argument made here is that innovative curatorial practices present opportunities for deconstructing and unsettling the tainted museological practices inherited from the colonial period. In terms of museological practice, these projects and the associated activities point to the need for an alternative museology – one that embraces local knowledge and custodians not merely as subjects of study or sources of information but as active players in curatorial practices. Through such participatory methodologies the museum can support multi-directional content that provides opportunities for diverse co-produced visitor experiences (Simon 2009).

We posit that for many African museums burdened with collections uprooted from communities during the colonial era, a "decolonial" museology that engenders a level of self-representation is a necessity, where previously marginalised knowledge can challenge colonially derived curatorial practices and reconnect objects with communities from which they were accumulated (Mignolo 2000, 2009, 2011). Thus, in many post-colonial nations, sharing power with indigenous communities in the making of museum exhibitions is a new methodology that should be used to pluralise, democratise and decolonize relations (Schmidt 2009; Onciul 2015). This is due to the fact that there is a paradoxical duality on the role of museums as key sites for the postcolonial debate, because on one hand they embody colonial narratives and on the other have the ability to decolonize the history of former colonial states (Onciul 2015: 26). To decolonize the museum simply means a proper representation of people spoken about rather than listened to. Community engagement has become a popular decolonial museological strategy that is being used in researching and designing new exhibitions. On the whole, decolonized methodologies can be applied to the museum institution by embracing the so-called unofficial narratives from non-experts and promoting an understanding of how to listen and pay attention to subaltern voices (Bugarin 2009; Harrison 2009; Ndlovu 2009; Schmidt 2009; Segobye 2009).

Today, across the global networks of heritage sites, museums and galleries, the importance of communities to the interpretation and conservation of heritage is increasingly being recognized (Watson 2007; Onciul et al. 2017). All over the world, the work that museums do, and particularly their role not just as storehouses of curiosities, has been a highlight for several decades. For instance, ethnographic museums, whose collections were accumulated from the so-called colonized world, have been rethinking the essence of what it means to hold such collections and how to deal with issues around new forms of representation and considerations for repatriation and restitution. The notion of museums as social institutions that must serve the interests of diverse audiences has also taken centre stage in museographic practices. Instead of regarding museums as clear and irrefutable senders of messages, the inclusion of multiple voices is being called for and museums are being pushed to adopt social missions. In so many ways, museums are also being challenged to give up on their authoritarian voice of control and allow the public or communities to speak for themselves, henceforth making them less of temples and more of forums of interaction (Hutchison 2013). Museums all over the world are becoming socially responsible in their curatorial and public programming and are responding to social issues affecting communities (Silverman 2010; Bautista 2013). For this reason, Karp, Kramer and Lavine (1992: 12) argue that "the best way to think about the changing relations between museums and communities is to think about how the *audience*, a passive entity, becomes the *community*, an active agent." It is also realistic to argue that museums can provide an enabling forum that empowers community members to actively engage and take control of their future (Sandell 2002: 7).

However, the interface between museums and communities has not always been a straight line. Many questions have been asked about the nature of communities, and the various ways in which museums can engage with these communities (Watson 2007; McCarthy 2016). What has been made clear is that museum practices are influenced by several political and power imperatives, and that museums themselves have always been purveyors of lopsided power relationships in community engagement, where the power of the museum institution and that of its authorized curatorial practices marginalize that of local communities (Hooper-Greenhill 1989, 1992; Karp and Lavine 1991; Karp, Kreamer and Levine 1992; Bennett 1995). As advocated by McCarthy (2016), it is crucial to always examine the different ways in which communities participate in heritage projects, (to) question the benefits, costs and limitations of community engagement. Given the histories of museum establishment in colonial Africa and the way these institutions have become part of postcolonial societies, it is important to look at how notwithstanding their colonial past, museums have charted new and emergent forms of relationships with the diversity that postcolonial societies espouse to champion. There has been emerging work on this idea – that of African museums taking new roles in postcolonial societies (Oyo 1994; Abungu 2001, 2002, 2006; Murray and Witz 2014).

Theoretically, there have been many interesting concepts that have been suggested to help us in understanding this new imperative and in positioning how museums can be active social institutions working in close relationship with local communities. Globally, various approaches have been suggested for the practices of museums and communities. For many countries, museums have increasingly been promoting their postcolonial status through inclusionist programs in exhibitions, shared curatorship, and use of collections. Where there are indigenous stakeholders, we have seen an unprecedented improvement in the empowerment of source communities in the management, use and presentation of their patrimony in museums (Boast 2011). These range from the idea of new museology (Vergo 1989), to James Clifford's (2007) idea of museums as "contact zones," to more works that have foregrounded the role of museums in social inclusion. The concept of the contact zone has allowed museums to evolve beyond easily definable geographical arenas of interaction into becoming places for dialogue and intercultural relations (Clifford 2007). According to Peers and Brown (2003: 5), "artefacts function as 'contact zones' – as sources of knowledge and as catalysts for new relationships – both within and between these communities." Elsewhere, Onciul (2015) moved a step further and proposed for what he calls the engagement zone, which is a physical and conceptual space in which participants interact when individuals from different groups enter. Within this engagement zone, the boundary between insider and outsider becomes blurred and temporary boundary crossings are affected (Onciul 2015). Engaging with communities can also allow museums to become places that support living indigenous cultural practices rather than being storage houses for disused objects. Using the engagement zone as a methodology in a museum can potentially transform as well as indigenize curatorial practices (Onciul 2015). Geographical distance should no longer separate the object and the subject but instead museums are striving to connect with communities from where their collections originated from (Shelton 2013; Wood and Latham 2013).

The idea of a "new museology" (Vergo 1989) is also a discourse around the social and political roles of museums that encourages new communication and new styles of expression in contrast to classic, collections-centred museum models. According to Watson (2007: 13), "if we understand 'old museology' to be characterised by an emphasis on the professional collection, documentation and interpretation of objects, then 'new museology' is community focused with emphasis on community needs." Thus, the relationship between source communities and museums is amplified in new museology in which the sources communities become equal partners as well as controlling agents (Message 2013). Aspects of new museology have included questioning and deconstructing the Eurocentric idea of museums as storehouses, deconstructing power relations between museums and the communities that they serve as well as a more active role for the public as both visitors and controllers of the curatorial function (Stam 1993). These approaches reflect greater awareness of the social and political role of museums and encompass meaningful community participation in curatorial practices (McCall and Gray 2014). They question traditional museum approaches to issues of value, meaning, control, interpretation, authority and authenticity. These challenges have implications for both internal operations and external relations of museums (Stam 1993). Recent works talk of museums making "authentic connections" with communities (Kadoyama 2018) or the idea of a museum as a "third place" (McCarthy 2016). There has been a paradigm shift where museums are now making attempts not only to address their colonial outlook but to take up new museological practices which seek to increase relevance through public engagement, participation and more inclusive forms of representation. According to Hutchison (2013: 145), "new museology is one way of describing a body of practical and theoretical museum work that takes account of the way museums position cultures and social identities in their collections and exhibitions and of the way they interact with their publics." New museology has a particular interest in democratic and inclusive practices that involves developing collaborative relationships with diverse groups and audiences which makes it a suitable decolonising method.

In examining the key components of the museum–community relationship, Margaret Kadoyama (2018) advocates for an accessible and inclusive approach to museum management and focuses on the role of museum leadership in fostering and deepening community relationships. McCarthy (2016) also talks of museums as "third places – environments other than work or home that often hold special meaning for visitors and may contribute to feelings of attachment to community. He further argues that in order for the museum to become viable into the future it must transition from a place where patrons visit occasionally to becoming an integral part of the surrounding community. Writing in an interesting blog "Savage Minds" in a piece entitled *The Anthropologist in the Museum: The Museum as Community*, Dustin Oneman (2012) states that "....what makes a museum a museum is that it's social, and that it's an institution- as a social phenomenon... a point of connection for a community of visitors, researchers, curators and other staff, and even subjects. And as an institution, that connection, that web of social relationships, is a structured one."[1] The idea of "the participatory museum" has also been proposed, where "planning, exhibition development, and administration are done not for a community but with or even in a community" (McCarthy 2016; Simon 2016).

This emerging work reflects on notions such as scholarship, community, participation and collaboration, which are sometimes deployed in tokenist ways. These works address practical concerns over what happens when museums put community-minded principles into practice (see Modest and Golding 2013). However, in spite of all these diverse approaches well advocated in museum studies literature, what still lacks in a substantial way are empirical studies of how these notions have been applied, and to what degree of success around the world – certainly not much from the African continent. For instance, in relation to the "new museology," Stam (1993) effectively challenges the extent to which these have been put into practice in many museums and cautions us that "a great deal of museological literature assumes that as a result of this rethinking of the purposes of museums, real change has occurred in both the understanding of museum functions and the activities that museums undertake. There has, however, been relatively little analysis of actual museum practice to assess the extent to which changes have actually lived up to the assumptions of the 'new museology' across the museums sector as a whole."[2]

For the Southern African context, McCarthy's (2016) argument that critiques the binary approaches to museum-community relations is quite useful. The author rightly observes that the dominant literature of museum studies and related fields is full of critiques of museums as powerhouses of social inequality or engines of public good. The emphasis is rather put on the notion that in spite of their lopsided power intricacies, and for postcolonial Africa, emerging from their histories and structures, museums can still be understood as places where cultures meet, negotiate, translate and intermingle (McCarthy 2016). In acknowledging and dealing with the tainted archives drawn from their colonial past, museums can foreground new curatorial strategies to bridge that gap. As proposed by McCarthy, in terms of knowledge contribution to literature on museums, the approach of highlighting new and emergent strategies addresses a significant gap in the available literature, exploring some of the complex issues arising from recent approaches to collaboration between museums and their communities (McCarthy 2016). However, while some curators are happy to allow visitors to temporarily act as curators, some are critical about the way in which being an expert is portrayed in these activities, feeling that their expertise is trivialized. Some have even argued that too much emphasis on social services is dangerous for the museum because it renders them "no longer museums as such" and represents a threat to museums' traditional activities of collecting, conservation, research and displaying (Silverman 2010; Iervolino 2013).

Decolonial museums: African museums challenging their own past

That a lot of African museums established during the colonial era face challenges of relevancy within their local communities is not debatable (Munjeri, 1990; Abungu, L. 2005). What is debatable is what strategies to adopt when dealing with the "colonial taint" that still affects museums in Africa. Large museums all over the world adhere to museological models developed in Europe during the nineteenth century and gradually modified over the twentieth century to fit in with the principles and standards of research, culture and taste of the countries concerned (de Varine 2005). The development of museums coincided with the spread of colonialism and imperialism and became part of a system that validated and justified oppression, dispossession and racial prejudice, where the study, collection and presentation of local cultures were seen as a key aspect of exerting power and control over locals (Said 1985; Dubow 1995, 2006; Foucault 1998; Lord 2006). In the colonial museum, the non-European world, disentangled from its cultural context, was represented in ethnographic and natural history museums that objectified vernacular traditions (Anderson 1983; Mignolo 2011). As elsewhere in the colonial world, museums in Africa are a product of Western modernity and over time they deployed ethnocentric approaches in knowledge production. The intellectual traditions complemented by biased museum representation marginalised the knowledge systems of the local populace from where most museum materials were collected. In the postcolonial era, this long history of classification, categorisation and interpretation which looked at cultures in colonised spaces either as curiosities or as intellectual subjects has created a situation in which these museums have to constantly struggle for relevance.

In recent years, decoloniality has been propounded as an alternative epistemological approach to deconstructing hegemony of Western/European in the production and circulation of knowledge (Mignolo 2000, 2011). This is framed with the understanding that collecting practices of the nineteenth century were always associated with violence and dispossession and that museums like universities and other research institutions in the colonial world "…. originating in the 16th century with the emergence of Atlantic commercial circuits, had and still have a role to play in the colonisation of knowledge and being" (Mignolo 2011: 72). While the call to "decolonise" the museums is not necessarily new, in Southern Africa the current fervent emergence of movements that use this term or approach in challenging the established structures of power is something that is indeed fascinating. It calls for attention and demands established institutions to rethink their strategies in dealing with the marginalised, opening spaces for increased inclusion and acceptance of difference.

But what does taking a decolonial approach to museum practice mean? While there is no established body of work on this yet, there is a growing collection of works that critique the inherited museum practices and propose the necessity of dealing with the colonial hangover of museums (Hooper-Greenhill 1989, 1992; Bennett 1995; Foucault 1998; Lord 2006). For instance, in his work on decoloniality, Walter Mignolo strongly argues that museums have always taken a central role in "reproducing the rhetoric of modernity, and the logic of coloniality," and he proposes what he calls "epistemic and aesthetic disobedience" (Mignolo 2011: 72; see also Mignolo 2000, 2009). The suggestions highlight the importance of creating spaces for local knowledge, what some have termed "knowledge at the borderlines," "disciplines on the frontier" or "information at the margins" (Haber and Gnecco 2007; Haber 2012; Gnecco 2013). Incorporating knowledge and experiences from the previously marginalised local communities has a potential for freeing the colonial museum from being seen as "… a space of difference, in which the relations between elements of a culture are suspended, neutralized, or reversed … whose power to collect and display objects is a function of capitalism and imperialism" (Lord 2006: 11; see also Hooper-Greenhill 1989, 1992; Bennett 1995; Foucault 1998).

After political independence in Sub-Saharan Africa, most public and national museums established in colonial times have continued to reproduce the prevailing modern episteme which appropriates or annihilates the "other" (Davison 1990, 2001, 2005; Ucko 1994; Corsane 2004). The decolonisation of the museum often happens through a merging of expert or museum-based curatorial methods and community-based practices where local interlocutors critically engage with collections and the structures of existing museums, "questioning the mechanisms of acquisition, selection, representation, interpretation, and appreciation" (L'Internationale Online 2015: 5). Attempts are being made by most museums to include members of the community in their galleries by making their stories part of the exhibitions – a move from the passive voice of expertise to authored polyvocal exhibits (Onciul 2015).

In attempts to rid the challenges of history, alternative museological practices have been called for. In 2015, L'Internationale produced an interesting report of case studies of various approaches from across the world. Entitled "Decolonising Museums," the report states that "decolonising" means:

> ... both resisting the reproduction of colonial taxonomies, while simultaneously vindicating radical multiplicity. ... understanding the situation museums are in, critically and openly, and identifying those moments that already indicate a different type of practice that overcomes or resists the colonial conditioning. (L'Internationale Online 2015: 5)

For the museums the term "decolonising" a museum may be construed to suggest the return to a pristine state "before" colonialism. Conversely, the notion acknowledges what Mignolo terms a colonial matrix of power, since the practice of collecting and classifying objects is deeply embedded in colonialism itself which created the museum institution as we know it today (Mignolo 2011). It acknowledges that knowledge practices born and entrenched during the colonial era prevail and muddle present practices, and that museum practice and the power imbalance that was once installed through colonisation still lingers today. Museums, through processing of interpretation, classification and display still have power, and it is this power that can be deconstructed by adopting innovative curatorial shifts that begin to change the institution's own history and practices. This approach resonates well with call for addressing issues on the relevance of African museums and increasing call for local communities' participation in new museological practices. It is important to note that the focus is not on the dismantling, the decentring the role of the museum in Africa or on portraying the ethnographic collections in African museums as dead and irrelevant archives. Rather, there has to be a revisioning of museum practices by foregrounding the agency of the ethnographic collections themselves. Regardless of the circumstances under which the ethnographic materials were accumulated into a colonial collection, a few objects and collections show that they still have potential to emerge and provoke new discussions, interpretations and new ways of display and handling.

While in many former colonial museums the narratives around these objects are still centred around the collectors, an argument is made for highlighting new forms of movement and circulation. Embracing and giving space to emerging players and the forms of knowledge and practices from the non-experts engender a new form of curation. A decolonial approach foregrounds the role of local communities in the reinterpretation and remaking of colonial collections, a relook at the collections that deconstruct, and challenges the entrenched curatorial practices. The approach seeks to unsettle the perception of a museum as an institution of aesthetic and epistemic control by "letting muted objects speak" (L'Internationale Online 2015: 5).

Continent-wide, there have been several initiatives to improve the operation of museums. For instance, the International Council of Museums (ICOM) has, since the 1960s, put up projects and programmes to support the development of museums in Africa. Since the mid-1980s, the International Centre for the Study of the Preservation and Restoration of Cultural Property (ICCROM), an intergovernmental organization dedicated to the preservation of cultural heritage worldwide through training, information, research, cooperation and advocacy programmes, has been facilitating capacity building programmes on heritage conservation across Africa. The African International Council of Museums (AFRICOM), though it had a difficult development trajectory, was started as a programme of the ICOM.[3] Outside of these initiatives that seek to improve the administrative, functional and financial aspects of museums' growth on the African content should be shifts in the thinking around what it is that museums must do and what messages they have to project in the new environments, particularly in dealing with local communities. This chapter highlights some recent developments in the museums in Zimbabwe and how a few objects have presented platforms for new approaches to museum practice.

A vital element of emerging work from Africa is the increasing call for theorizing museum practice in Africa (Pastor 2000). Literature on museums in Africa is skewed in favour of South Africa, where the post-1994 imperative for change in the heritage and museum sector spurred a considerable amount of academic attention (Davison 2005; Dubin 2006). By documenting and analysing practical projects within museums in Africa, one can contribute to theories on further understanding the nature of museums as institutions and their role in the public sphere (Witcomb 2007; Witcomb and Message 2015). Empirical insights from an African perspective are important especially because the last few decades have seen interesting developments in museums on the continent. In the literature, attention to museum developments on the African continent has been scant, with the few that exist failing to adequately address some of the creative ways that museums in postcolonial Africa (outside of South Africa) have traversed their roles and created a different kind of museological practice in response to the changing political, sociocultural and economic aspects of their society.

Substantial work, but perhaps not enough, has been done on the role of museums on the African continent. Very little exists in terms of the development of museums and the role they have continued to play in other parts of Africa. However, a substantial amount of work on African museums has been done since the 1990s, such as that by ICOM (1995), who as early as 1991 were concerned with "What Museums for Africa? Heritage in the Future" (ICOM 1991), or fostering financial and administrative autonomy within African museums (ICOM 1995; Négri 1995). AFRICOM, a non-governmental, autonomous and pan-African organization of museums was created in October 1999.[4] Other international activities have included ICCROM's capacity building in museum collection conservation through Prevention for Museums in Africa (PREMA) (Labi 2018).[5] Amid all this, there has been substantial call for the transformation of the museum sector on Africa where, for example, museums are seen as "arenas for dialogue or confrontation" (Abungu 2001: 15–18) or seen as contributing to "opening up of new frontiers…in the 21st Century" (Abungu 2002; 2006). In other countries in Africa, interesting developments in the past few years have included the important role of museums and education in Botswana through their popular mobile museum educational outreach programme, Zebra (Rammapudi 2004); an increase in community-based museums in countries like Zimbabwe (Chikozho 2015); the proliferation of living museums among remote rural communities in Namibia (Akuupa 2012; Dürrschmidt 2012) and the vital role played by non-state-based organizations, such as the Namibian Museum Association, in museum development and capacity building among relatively less resourced museums. In Eastern Africa, Ugandan and Kenyan museums have continued to contribute to community healing among conflict regions of Uganda (Abiti 2012, 2018; Tindi 2012), while in central Africa, the contentious Royal Palace museums of the Grassland of Cameroon have emerged strongly as part of Cameroonian cultural representation (Forni 2012; Oberhofer 2018). Across the continent, museums continue to make efforts to integrate themselves with community economic and social needs. For example, museums in Zambia and Malawi, which are dealing with challenges of increasing urban migration (Mudenda 2002, 2010; Maluwa 2006).

More recent work has spurred discussions in Africa focusing on the new and emerging relationships and cooperation between African and European museums and questions of repatriations (Laely et al. 2018). There is thus a renewed interest in African museums on various levels, including their changing roles within their communities as well as their relationships with museums in other parts of the world. Museums in southern Africa are currently deeply involved in conversation and contestation on the curatorship and repatriation of human remains in museums amid increasing requests to repatriate and return human remains in African museums as well as the remains of Africans in other countries (Legassick and Rassool 2000; Sealy 2003; Rasool 2015). This was encapsulated in debates following recent (August 2018) hand-over of human remains of the Herero and Nama people that were acquired for racially-tinged scientific experiments during Germany's brutal colonial legacy in Namibia and had been kept in German museums and universities for decades. Kenya's processes of planning and implementing change within the museum sector in the National Museums and Monuments of Kenya represent a common concern for change, relevancy and suitability among museums across the continent.

The museum in Africa: agents for social change?

Perhaps one of the biggest questions facing the museum community in Africa is whether museums in Africa can be effective agents of social change. Their first challenge is that of dealing with the knowledge production and representation practices drawn from and largely influenced by European modernity. More importantly, attention has to be paid to how African museums can be transformed into spaces that engender, appreciate and promote multivocality and accept the place of different ways of knowing in knowledge production and representation. In attempting to do this, the concept of decoloniality has an irresistible appeal, especially the way in which decoloniality in a museum challenges the universalisation of European modernity and authority of interpretation (Laely et al. 2018). We present decoloniality from a perspective of looking at how the Mutare Museum developed powerful alternative epistemologies and methods rooted in community engagement, participation, collaboration, consultation and negotiation.

Mutare Museum used holistic approaches which prioritised non-binary or non-bifurcated divisions between tangible and intangible objects. We argue that this museum devised a broad social practice where objects are more than purveyors of information but also of agency and affects (Gosden 2005; Golding 2013). In presenting decolonial strategies that undergirded collaborative programmes at Mutare Museum, we sharply look at exhibition co-curation, community collaboration, participation and the hosting of community festivals. Henceforth, we argue that decoloniality at Mutare Museum delinked colonial ethnographic classifications by constructing a praxis that was collaborative in allowing for alternative ways of knowing, thinking, being and doing. Our case studies in this book highlight a number of decolonial strategies that Mutare Museum initiated by way of involvement, mutuality, reciprocity, exchange, equal partnership, outreach, collaboration and shared responsibility with the community. Being an agent of change meant that the museum was able to solve a number of community problems rather than merely being a passive presenter of the past. Community collaboration in this book is presented as a strategy used by the museum to delve into a number of social challenges to make a difference.

At the same time, community self-representation in museum activities has of late been influential in re-balancing the relationship between museums and communities. What do decolonial museum practices look like? Vawda (2019: 78) argues that "decolonization means taking the concept of sharing seriously, allowing for the multivalent voices and multi-authorial possibilities to emerge and strengthen, in documenting and curating the complex and specific histories, cultures, scientific and everyday practices of people." It has also been argued that community participation, outreach, in-reach, collaborative processes and co-creation as decolonial strategies are bringing profound epistemological and museological innovation to museums (Sandahl 2019: 104). Elsewhere, Simon's (2010) work has been quite influential in clearing the way for providing practical, participatory strategies that can be embraced by museums by working with the community through a deep investment of time, passion and commitment. By using empirical examples drawn from co-curating the diamond mining exhibition, the hosting of a cultural festival and collaborative site management projects, we illuminate how these programmes repositioned Mutare Museum in its new role as a decolonial agent for social change. We argue that by becoming an important community anchor institution, Mutare

Museum transcended beyond its colonial outlook whose preoccupation was underpinned by gathering of collections, conservation and presentation of cultural heritage to the public into becoming an interactive space where day-to-day challenges are discussed. Elsewhere in the world, museums are taking on new social responsibilities by reaching out for greater public participation through outreach programmes. This is being achieved through co-creation and working together with communities to design a course of action rooted in from a shared vision, and in the process effecting social change (Janes and Sandell 2019).

We also argue that decolonial museologies should strive to engender a level of self-representation where previously marginalised knowledge can challenge colonially derived curatorial practices and reconnect objects with communities from where they were accumulated. Although these objects may appear mundane within ethnographic classifications, they have individual biographies and carry with them important meanings connected to their ritual and cultural functions located in societies of origin (Arero 2005; Verges 2014; Golding and Modest 2013; McCarthy 2019). Henceforth, to decolonise the museum means there is a need for a mindset change and paradigm shift that must first come to terms with the harsh realities of colonisation with the admission that museums were beneficiaries of these past injustices (Abungu 2019). On the other hand, Sandahl (2019: 75) argues that "decolonising museum curating involves decoding museum collections from the colonial meanings in which they have been cut off, displayed and decontextualized from where they had once belonged, and in which have been categorised, labelled and transposed into the alien binary hierarchies of Western rationalism and the value systems of colonialism and imperialism." Museums in Africa were and still are in most cases colonizing spaces which are viewed by local communities as intimately tied to the process of colonisation. Similarly, Catlin-Legutko (2019: 44) argues that "decolonisation means, at minimum, sharing governance structures and authority for the documentation and interpretation of native culture." Decolonising practices are collaborative, which means when an idea for a project or initiative is first conceived there should be a conversation with the local community to ensure that it is a story for which curators have been given the green light to pursue (Catlin-Legutko, 2019: 41). Effective collaboration needs to occur at the beginning and be threaded throughout the life of the project, as we demonstrate in this book. Decolonising museum practices also entails privileging voices and perspectives of local communities in exhibition development. Within the decolonisation framework, indigenous ontologies and epistemologies are blended with cross-cultural collaborations between the museum and community-driven initiatives (McCarthy 2019: 41).

In many African countries, museums are still imbricated in colonialism as sites of deep epistemological unjust practices. The act of appropriating objects, recording their provenance, dislocating them from their original contexts and ignoring their social biographies constituted an act of epistemic violence. Epistemic violence is regarded here as violence exerted through knowledge and as an element of domination (Vawda 2019). Epistemic decolonisation then involves the construction of a new social condition of knowledge underpinned by collaborating with communities that were previously marginalised and considered as the "other." In recent years, decoloniality has been propounded as an alternative epistemological approach to deconstructing hegemony of Western/European culture in the production and circulation of knowledge in the global south (Mignolo 2011). This is framed with the understanding that collecting practices of the nineteenth century were always associated with violence and dispossession and that museums, like universities and other research institutions in the colonial world ".... originating in the 16th century with the emergence of Atlantic commercial circuits, had and still have a role to play in the colonisation of knowledge and being" (Mignolo 2011: 72).

While the call to "decolonise" the museums is not necessarily new, in Africa the current fervent emergence of movements that use this term or approach in challenging the established structures of power is something that is indeed fascinating. It calls for attention and demands established institutions to rethink their strategies in dealing with marginalised peoples, opening spaces for increased inclusion and acceptance of difference. Drawing from activities of Mutare Museum in Eastern Zimbabwe, we look at how inherited colonial legacies are being decolonised through new forms of engagement where issues such as economic livelihood, poverty, displacement, climate change and education are actively articulated. We argue that active community involvement in the creation of cultural capital at this museum was not simply premised on mere consultations but transcended to active working collaborative programmes with shared decision making and shared outcomes.

Museums in Zimbabwe: brief history and context

The national museums in Zimbabwe were built in the late nineteenth to mid-twentieth century, along with the expansion of colonial rule. Museum construction was an integral part of the expansion of

European capital and the establishment of political control, aspects that were always associated with racial prejudice as well as social and epistemic violence. Colonialism profoundly impacted many aspects of life, and in the case of museums it influenced collecting practices, the scope of their narratives and curatorial cultures (Ariese-Vandemeulebroucke 2018). Museum making in early Rhodesia (now Zimbabwe) were at the impetus of the mining interests of the British South African Company (BSAC) – a company formed to take over the natural and mineral resources as well as land in Southern Africa. The BSAC's expansionist agenda in southern Africa was associated with a growing number of colonial scholars/scientists whose interests were to study, collect and appropriate the natural facets of the new colony. They desired to build up a base of basic scientific archive for perpetuating the control of resources and entrenching colonial political power. The work of corporate companies, interest groups and pseudo-scientists such as BSAC and the Rhodesian Scientific Association (RSA) dominated the efforts at establishing the first museums in early Rhodesia.

Over the years, as the settler political economy entrenched itself in the new place, legislation was passed to control the "heritage" of the new colony, pushed by the fascination of the international scientific community over the Great Zimbabwe archaeological site/shrine in the southern parts of the country. By 1903, the Rhodesian Museum in Bulawayo and the Queen Victoria Memorial Museum in Salisbury had already started collecting materials. The activities of these museums were buttressed by a number of legislations passed by the young government. The legal pronouncements were meant to protect the country's rich nature and archaeological sites, the latter of which had already grabbed international attention. By 1937, the legislation had effectively allowed for the state control of all monuments and museums. From the 1930s, this legal appropriation of the natural, historical and archaeological aspects of the country was entrenched in the 1970s with the passing of the National Museums and Monuments Act (1972), giving the state firmer control on the country's natural and cultural heritage. Alongside this, the assembling and making of museum collections was carried out mostly by missionaries, colonial officials, the police, enthusiasts and a growing number of scientists and intellectuals whose efforts filled the museum vaults most times with poorly documented material culture from the African communities.

Regardless of the expectations for change in museum practices, after 1980 when Zimbabwe attained political independence, there was very little change outside of the few structural and administrative changes that were made (Ucko,1994). Museums were criticised for failing to change the biases inherent in colonial museums (Garlake 1982; Mazel and Ritchie 1994). In response to increasing criticism of the lack of change within the inherited museums, the government made attempts to introduce new types of museums which were expected to serve the interests of mainly rural communities. Financial and material support was provided for site museums, interpretive centres and community museums constructed around archaeological sites and near local communities.

In the early to mid-1980s, the government supported a project that sought to create what were called "Culture Houses" in each of the 54 districts across the country. These places would be used as centres for cultural activities but did not roll out to any district except only one (Ucko 1981, 1994). In the late 1990s there was also an emphasis on community museums, which were expected to offer space for the cultures of underrepresented minority groups. In 2004, the BaTonga Museum, presenting the life, history and culture of the Tonga people in Zimbabwe, became the first community museum to be officially opened. Other examples of community museums in the country that were established after independence in 1980 are the Nambya Community Museum in Hwange, the Old Bulawayo Open Air Museum in Bulawayo and the Marange Community Museum in Mutare. Community museums were seen as alternatives to the colonial museums, where collection and curatorial activities would be shared with local communities. The proliferation of community museums in Zimbabwe became an effective way through which previously marginalised groups preserved and interpreted their own cultures (Chipangura and Chipangura 2020). It has also been argued that community museums represent an empirical illustration of how the museum practice can be decolonised because they embrace collaborations with community members (Chipangura and Chipangura 2020; Taruvinga and Ndoro 2003). This is because a decolonial perspective represented by a community museum acknowledges that objects are not mundane but rather represent the coming together of a multiplicity of factors, and it also questions the binary division between tangible and intangible heritage knowledge production. There is also a recognised difference between a community museum and a national museum in terms of function. National museums are highly specialised and secular, driven by academic and professional aspirations (Stanley 2008). In Africa, most national museums still function as places where various cultures mix and where the identities of nations are formulated. In contrast, a community museum is locally accented,

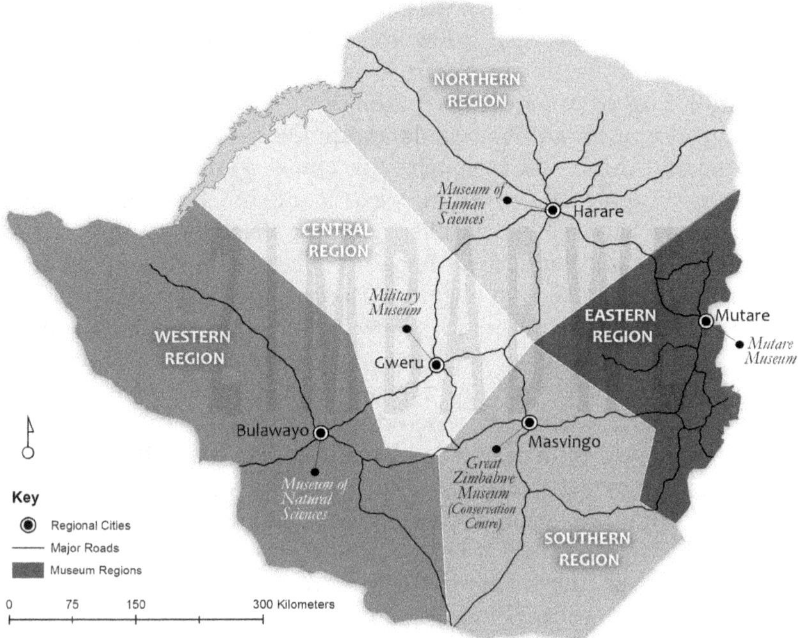

Figure 0.2 Locations of museums in Zimbabwe. Njabulo Chipangura.

self-announcing and self-conscious (Kingdon 2005). In light of these differences, community museums in Africa can be regarded as integral to decolonial methodologies embraced by local people in response to exclusion or misrepresentations in national museums (Chipangura and Chipangura 2020). This view is supported by Boast (2011), who succinctly argues that due to frustrations with engagements with existing national museums and a complete insignificance of national museums to the community indigenous people are creating their own centres of collecting, performance and presentation (Figure 0.2).

Meanwhile, Mutare Museum is the eastern branch of NMMZ situated in Eastern Zimbabwe and is the national collector of transport objects and antiquities. The other museums in the country are the Zimbabwe Museum of Human Sciences (Harare), which specializes in human sciences; the Natural History Museum (Bulawayo), which specialises in natural sciences; the Military Museum (Gweru), which specialises in militaria, aviation and mining; and the Great Zimbabwe Museum (Masvingo), which specializes in archaeology and heritage management. The Mutare Museum has been collecting and exhibiting objects and materials associated with the development of transport in Zimbabwe. Though it has a few archaeological, natural history and ethnographic collections, its main focus has been collecting items representing European modernity in the colony. Vestiges of motor cars, railway equipment and household antiquities form the core of its collection and exhibitions. In spite of this colonial archive, this museum has recently deployed active strategies that are redefining its roles, and is acting as an agent for social change. These strategies represent a new form of museum practice in Zimbabwe, one that is no longer hinged on the internal possession of collections but by an external consideration of the needs of communities served (Weil 2003). Beyond its collections, by undertaking and focusing on collaborative programmes that have a bearing on community aspirations, the museum has managed to counterbalance the authorised discourse which was driven by its previous sole purpose of managing static collections collected during the colonial era. As a result, and in line with its new vision of activism, the Mutare Museum has transformed into a multivocal space for critical dialogue in which it is now curating both stories and objects.

Looking back, the history of the Mutare Museum (formerly Umtali Museum) is inextricably interwoven with that of the Umtali Society (Broadley 1966). The Umtali Society came into being as a committee of the Southern Rhodesia Hunters and Game Preservation Association in October 1953. This society was established for the purpose of inaugurating and fostering interest in the establishment of a museum in Umtali (now Mutare City). The society accumulated and displayed the first collections of historical and natural objects in January 1956 which persuaded the municipality to provide a temporary home for the museum (Broadley 1966). It was only in November 1957 that the Umtali Municipality granted the association some space in an old hostel, allowing them to exhibit on a semi-permanent basis (Broadley 1966). By mid-1958, about 500 people were visiting the museum each month but the museum had no funds for further development, which led them to approach the trustees of National Museums and Monuments of Rhodesia to take over. Sir Edgar Whitehead officially opened the museum in November 1958 after having secured grants from the government and Umtali Municipality. Captain E. F. Boultbee was then appointed Honorary Curator of the Umtali Museum on 1 September 1959 (Broadley 1966).

The trustees realised that the existing building was unsuitable for a museum, and with the help of the Umtali Museum Society it raised funds for a new museum building. The new museum building was officially opened by Sir Alfred Beit on 13 September 1964 (Broadley

1966). When it opened its doors to the public, the museum had displays in antiquities, transport, botany and geology. Additional displays of ethnographic and archaeological objects were later put in the Beit Gallery. Thus, the museum's origins are steeped in the interests of a small group of white settlers whose interests were narrow and devoted to their own purposes. This, in the divided colonial period, served the interests of selected white dwellers in the city, excluding the majority of black inhabitants. Therefore, as illustrated, the formation of Mutare Museum and many other museums throughout Africa is closely linked with the phenomenon of colonialism (Arinze 1995; Anderson 1991; Bennett 1995). These museums were formed as a result of colonial encounters. They share a common history in terms of their development in that they tend to be the by-products of colonialism and are twentieth century creations – a period in which their formation came as a result of European imperialism. Since most museums in Africa are colonial in character, they are usually divorced from their surroundings which contain nuclear elements of African people's traditions, ways of praying, and use of the same objects that were appropriated from them and deposited into the museum (Andah 1997; Mawere 2015). In Africa, most national museums are conceived of as offshoots of colonial legacies and are still obsessed with an ethnographic, historic and folkloric image of societies and pay little attention to history in its various social, political and economic aspects. They still continue to practice colonial museology given that a number of them still depict the histories and tastes of the Western society of conquerors and colonialists who established museums on the African soils after realising their [museums] value in the global market (Mawere 2015). Also argues that African museums are often associated with objects which are viewed as dead and lifeless because for too long objects on display have not been changed to reflect social and economic realities of their communities. Exhibitions at Mutare Museum had also been stagnant and biased towards colonialism such that many aspects of an independent Zimbabwe were ignored, hence the growing need to decolonise this museum.

Conclusion

The collaborative programmes foregrounded in this book point to innovative, new strategies being deployed by smaller museums in charting new trajectories in museum practice in Africa. In an ever-changing world, in a region thwarted by very specific challenges such as conflict, poverty, displacement, diseases and others, the museums cannot remain rooted in their colonial past. This book highlights merging notions and practices of museum-community relations in Africa, foreground issues around dealing with inherited pasts, power and inclusion in small museums. Research and museum practice in the last few decades have demonstrated the complex nature of the relationship between museums and communities (Watson 2007). One of the key questions has been how to find strategies for open and inclusive relationships between museums and communities. The collaborative programmes adopted by Mutare Museum help us in further understanding the various issues to be taken into consideration for inclusivity. From a methodological point of view, collaborations and participatory techniques that involved embracing community voices will inform key debates in this book. Conceptually, the case study of Mutare Museum contributes new knowledge on key discussions about how the museum practice in Africa can be decolonised through collaborative programmes that involve communities. The selected programmes question who the community is, who is included and excluded, and how power relations operate in the context of post-colonial museums seeking to engender inclusive relationships with a community. More importantly, we will look at how museum-community interfaces help in dealing with the challenges of the day – economic well-being, poverty, displacement, sensitive societal cultural practices, spirituality and others.

Notes

1 See Dustin (Oneman) (2012). The Anthropologist in the Museum: The Museum as Community. https://savageminds.org/2012/10/09/the-anthropologist-in-the-museum-the-museum-as-community/ (accessed 25/10/2018).
2 See New Museology Concepts https://evmuseography.wordpress.com/2015/01/24/new-museology-concepts/ (accessed 12/09/2018).
3 ICOM activities have included a number of projects and programmes such capacity building efforts, networking and awareness raising within African museums. Recent programmes include the Swedish-African Museum Programme (SAMP) and the West African Museums Programme (WAMP). AFRICOM was established to promote the development of museums on the African continent and currently has over 1500 museum professionals representing 240 museum institutions in 51 African countries and operating in the entire African regions of Central Africa, East Africa, the Indian Ocean Islands, North Africa, Southern Africa and West Africa (Amwinda 2012).
4 ICOM supported AFRICOM's foundations and was created in 1991 on the initiative of Alpha Oumar Konaré, then president of ICOM and president of the Republic of Mali. One of the first encounters on the

theme "What Museums for Africa? Heritage in the Future" was organised by ICOM in Lomé (Togo), while another focused on "Autonomy in African Museums" (ICOM 1991, 1995).

5 Preventive Conservation in Museums of Africa (PREMA) was a programme developed by the International Centre for the Study of the Preservation and Restoration of Cultural Property (ICCROM) for African museums south of the Sahara. Its aim was to establish before the year 2000 a network of African professionals capable of taking charge of the conservation of collections and the training of colleagues, thereby giving Sub-Saharan African museums tools for long-lasting development. PREMA led to the training of hundreds of museum professionals from more than forty African countries and ultimately to the creation of the first permanent African conservation organizations: Ecole du Patrimoine African (EPA) in Benin and the Centre for Heritage Development in Africa (CHDA) in Kenya (ICCROM 2009). Programs in West included the West African Museums Program (WAMP). The programs built professional capacity on the continent, strengthened key heritage organizations, and coordinated region-wide training (see http://www.getty.edu/foundation/initiatives/past/africa/index.html).

Bibliography

Abiti, N. A. (2012). Post-conflict memorial preservation for reconciliation and the promotion of peace: The case of the Pabbo Internal People's Displaced Camp Memorial. Paper presented at the *ICME-ICOM Annual Meeting*, Windhoek, Namibia, September 12–14, 2012.

Abiti, N. A. (2018). The Road to Reconciliation: Museum Practice, Community Memorial and Collaboration in Uganda. In T. Laely, M. Meyer and S. Ra (eds). *Museum Cooperation between Africa and Europe. A New Field for Museum Studies*. Kampala: Fountain Publishers/Bielefield, Transcript Verlag, pp. 83–98.

Abungu, G. (2001). Museums: Arenas for Dialogue or Confrontation. *ICOM News* 2: 15–18.

Abungu, G. (2002). Opening Up New Frontiers: Museums of the 21st Century. In P. U. Argren and S. Nyman (eds). *Museums 2000: Confirmation or Challenge.* Stockholm: ICOM Sweden and the Swedish Museum Association, pp. 37–43.

Abungu, G. (2006). Africa and Its Museums: Changing of Pathways? In B. T. Hoffman (ed). *Art and Cultural Heritage: Law, Policy, and Practice.* New York, NY: Cambridge University Press, pp. 386–393.

Abungu, G. O. (2019). Museums: Geopolitics, Decolonisation, Globalisation and Migration. *Museum International* 71 (281–282–281–282): 62–71.

Abungu, L. (2005). Museums and Communities in Africa: Facing the New Challenges. *Public Archaeology* 4 (2–3–2–3): 151–154.

Akuupa, M. U. (2012). Museums and Living Museums in Post-apartheid Namibia: A Critical Review. Paper presented at the *ICME-ICOM Annual Meeti*ng, Windhoek, Namibia, September 12–14, 2012.

Amwinda, F. (2012). The Role of AFRICOM in Museum Development in Relation to Human Rights. *Federation of International Human Rights Museums Conference*, International Slavery Museum, Liverpool, October, 8–10, 2012.

Anderson, B. (1983). *Imagined Communities: Reflections on the Origin and Spread of Nationalism*. London: Verso.

Anderson, B. (1991). *Imagined Communities: Reflections on the Origin and Spread of Nationalism*, Second Edition. London: Verso.

Arero, H. (2005). Tracing Contours of Creativity in Pastoralist Visual Culture. In H. Arero and Kingdon, Z (eds). *East African Contours: Reviewing Creativity and Visual Arts*. London: The Horniman Museum and Gardens, pp. 21–40

Ariese-Vandemeulebroucke, C. (2018). *The Social Museum in the Caribbean: Grassroots Heritage Initiatives and Community Engagement*. Leiden: Sidestone Press.

Arinze, E. (1995). The Training of Local Museum Stuff. In C. D. Ardouin and E. Arinze (eds). *Museums and the Community in West Africa*. Washington: Smithsonian Institution, pp. 35–44.

Bautista, S. S. (2013). *Museums in the Digital Age: Changing Meanings of Places, Community, and Culture*. New York: AltaMira Press.

Bennett, T. (1995). *The Birth of the Museum: History, Theory, Politics*. New York: Routledge.

Boast, R. (2011). Neocolonial Collaboration: Museum as Contact Zone Revisited. *Museum Anthropology* 34 (1–1): 56–70.

Broadley, D. (1966). History of Umtali Museum. *Rhodesian Science News* 8 (5–5): 1–30.

Bugarin, F. T. (2009). Embracing Many Voices as Keepers of the Past. In P. R. Schmidt (ed). *Postcolonial Archaeologies in Africa.* Santa Fe, NM: School for Advanced Research Press, pp. 193–210.

Catlin-Legutko, C. (2019). History That Promotes Understanding in a Diverse Society In J. B. Cole and L. L. Lott (eds). London: Rowman and Littlefield, pp. 41–48.

Chikozho, J. (2015). Community Museums in Zimbabwe as a Means of Engagement and Empowerment: Challenges and Prospects. In M. Mawere, H. Chiwaura and T.P. Thondhlana (eds). *African Museums in the Making: Reflections on the Politics of Material and Public Culture in Zimbabwe*. Bamenda: Langaa Publishing.

Chirikure, S. and Pwiti, G. (2008). Community Involvement in Archaeology and Cultural Heritage Management: An Assessment from Case Studies in Southern Africa and Elsewhere. *Current Anthropology Journal* 49 (3–3): 467–489.

Clifford, J. (2007). The Quai Branly in Process. *October* 120 (3–3): 3–23.

Corsane, G. (2004). Transforming Museums and Heritage in Postcolonial and Post-Apartheid South Africa: The Impact of Processes of Policy Formulation and New Legislation Social Analysis. *The International Journal of Anthropology* 48 (1–1): 515.

Davison, P. (1990). Ethnography and Cultural History in South African Museums. *African Studies* 49: 1.

Davison, P. (2001). Typecast: Representations of the Bushmen at the South African Museum. *Public Archaeology* 2: 3–20.

Davison, P. (2005). Museums and the Reshaping of Memory In G. Corsane (ed). *Heritage, Museums and Galleries: An Introductory Reader.* London: Routledge, pp. 184–194.

de Varine, H. (2005). Decolonising Museology. *ICOM News* 58 (3).

Dubin, S. (2006). *Transforming Museums: Mounting Queen Victoria in a Democratic South Africa.* New York: Palgrave.

Dubow, S. (1995). *Scientific Racism in South Africa.* Cambridge: Cambridge University Press.

Dubow, S. (2006). *A Commonwealth of Knowledge: Science, Sensibility, and White South Africa 1820–2000.* Oxford: Oxford University Press.

Dürrschmidt, K. (2012). Can Living Museums in Namibia be an Effective Way of Preserving Cultural Knowledge? Paper presented at the *ICME-ICOM Annual Meeting*, Windhoek, Namibia, September 12–14, 2012.

Forni, S. (2012). A Museum Fit for a King: Art, Heritage and Politics in the Cameroonian Grasslands. Paper presented at the *ICME-ICOM Annual Meeting*, Windhoek, Namibia, September 12–14, 2012.

Foucault, M. (1998). Different Spaces. In R. Hurley and M. Foucault (eds). *Essential Works of Foucault 1954–1984.* London: Penguin, pp. 175–185.

Fraser, J. (2019). A Discomforting Definition of Museum. *Curator: The Museum Journal* 62 (4–4): 501–504.

Garlake, P. S. (1982). Museums Remain Rooted in the Past. *Moto* 31–32

Gentles, S. J. and Jack, S. M. (2014). A Critical Approach to Reflexivity in Grounded Theory. *The Qualitative Report* 19(25): 1–14.

Gnecco, C. (2013). Digging Alternative Archaeologies. In A. González-Ruibal (ed). *Reclaiming Archaeology.* London: Routledge, pp. 67–78.

Golding, V. (2013). Museums, Poetics and Affect. *Feminist Review* 104 (1–1): 80–99.

Golding, V. and Modest, W. (eds). (2013.) *Museums and Communities, Curators, Collections and Collaboration*. Bloomsbury Academic.

Gosden, C. (2005). What Do Objects Want? *Journal of Archaeological Method and Theory* 12: 193–211.

Haber, A. F. (2012). Un-Disciplining Archaeology. *Archaeologies: Journal of the World Archaeological Congress* 8 (1–1): 55–65.

Haber, A. F. and Gnecco, C. (2007). Virtual Forum: Archaeology and Decolonization Archaeologies. *Journal of the World Archaeological Congress* 3 (3–3): 390–412.

Harrison, F. V. (2009). Reworking African (1st) Archaeology in the Postcolonial Period: A Sociocultural Anthropologist's Perspective. In P. R. Schmidt (ed). *Postcolonial Archaeologies in Africa.* Santa Fe, NM: School for Advanced Research Press, pp. 231–242.

Hooper-Greenhill, E. (1989). The Museum in the Disciplinary Society. In S. Pearce (ed). *Museum Studies in Material Culture.* London: Leicester University Press, pp. 61–72.

Hooper-Greenhill, E. (1992). *Museums and the Shaping of Knowledge*. London: Routledge.

Hutchison, M. (2013). Shared Authority: Collaboration, Curatorial Voice and Exhibition Design in Canberra, Australia. In V. Golding and W. Modest (eds). *Museums and Communities: Curators, Collections and Collaborations.* London: Bloomsbury, pp. 143–162.

ICCROM. (2009) *ICCROM Newsletter*. Rome: International Centre for the Study of the Preservation and Restoration of Cultural Property, October 2009.

ICOM. (1991). What Museums for Africa: Heritage in the Future. *Proceedings of ICOM Conference in Benin, Ghana and Togo*. ICOM.

ICOM. (1995). *Autonomy of Museums in Africa.* Paris: International Council of Museums.

Iervolino, S. (2013). Museums, Migrant Communities and Intercultural Dialogue in Italy. In V. Golding and W. Modest (eds). *Museums and Communities: Curators, Collections and Collaborations.* London: Bloomsbury, pp. 113–129.

Janes, R. and Sandell, R. (2019). Posterity Has Arrived: The Necessary Emergence of Museum Activism. In R. Janes and R. Sandell (eds). London: Routledge, pp. 1–23.

Kadoyama, M. (2018). *Museums Involving Communities Authentic Connections*, 1st Edition. New York: Routledge.

Karp, I., Kreamer, C. M. and Levine, S. (eds). (1992). *Museums and Communities: The Politics of Public Culture*. Smithsonian Books.

Karp, I. and Lavine, D. (eds). (1991). *Exhibiting Cultures: The Poetics and Politics of Museum Display*. Washington, DC: Smithsonian.

Kingdon, Z. (2005). Creative Frontiers: Sculptural Innovation and Social Transformation in East Africa. In H. Arero and Z. Kingdon (eds). *East African Contours: Reviewing Creativity and Visual Arts*. London: The Horniman Museum and Gardens, pp. 1–20.

Labi, K. A. (2018). New Considerations in Afro-European Museum Cooperation in Africa: The Examples of PREMA and Other Initiatives in Ghana. In T. Laely, M. Meyer and S. Ra (eds). *Museum Cooperation between Africa and Europe. A New Field for Museum Studies.* Kampala: Fountain Publishers/Bielefield, Transcript Verlag, pp. 165–178.

Laely, T., Meyer, M. and Schwere, R. (eds). (2018). *Museum Cooperation between Africa and Europe. A New Field for Museum Studies.* Kampala: Fountain Publishers/Bielefield, Transcript Verlag.

Legassick, M. and Rassool, C. (2000). *Skeletons in the Cupboard: South African Museums and the Trade in Human Remains 1907-1917*. Cape Town: South African Museum; Kimberley: McGregor Museum.

L'Internationale Online. (2015). *Decolonising Museums*. L'Internationale Books. Retrieved December 12, 2015 from www.internationaleonline.org

Lord, B. (2006). Foucault's Museum: Difference, Representation, and Genealogy. *Museum and Society* 4 (1–1): 11–14.

Macdonald, S. and Morgan, J. (2019). What Not to Collect? Post-Connoisseurial Dystopia and the Profusion of Things. In P. Schorch, C. McCarthy and E. Durr (eds). Manchester: Manchester University Press, pp. 29–43.

Maluwa, A. A. (2006). The Role of Museums in Addressing Community Needs in the 21st Century, *Paper presented for the conference Connections, Communities And Collections.* Miami Beach, FL. July 10–12, 2006.

Mazel, A. and Ritchie, G. (1994). Museums and Their Messages: The Display of the Pre and Early Colonial Past in the Museums of South Africa, Botswana and Zimbabwe. In P. G. Stone and B. L. Molyneaux (eds). *The Presented Past: Heritage, Museums and Education.* London: Routledge, pp. 225–236.

McCall, V. and Gray, C. (2014). Museums and the 'new museology': Theory, practice and organisational change. *Museum Management and Curatorship* 29 (1–1): 19–35.

McCarthy, C. (2016). Theorising Museum Practice through Practice: Theory Museum Studies as Intercultural Practice. In P. Burnard, E. Mackinlay and K. Powell (eds). *The Routledge International Handbook of Intercultural Arts Research*. London: Routledge.

McCarthy, C. (2019). Reconceptualizing Museology. In S. Knell (ed). London: Routledge, pp. 37–55.

Message, K. (2013). *Museums and Social Activism: Engaged Protests*. London: Routledge.

Message. K. (2018). *The Disobedient Museum: Writing at the Edge*. London: Routledge.

Mignolo, W. (2011). Museums in the Colonial Horizon of Modernity: Fred Wilson's Mining the Museum (1992). In J. Harris (ed). *Globalization and Contemporary Art*. Hoboken, NJ: Wiley-Blackwell, pp. 71–85.

Mignolo, W. D. (2000). *Local Histories/Global Designs: Coloniality, Subaltern Knowledge, and Border Thinking*. Princeton, NJ: Princeton University Press.

Mignolo, W. D. (2009). Epistemic Disobedience, Independent Thought and Decolonial Freedom. *Theory, Culture & Society* 26 (7/8–7/8): 159–81.

Mudenda, G. S. (2002). The Role of Museums in Rapidly Growing Cities: A Zambian Case. Paper presented at the *Conference High Expectations, but Low Funding: How do Poor Museums Meet Their Targets*? Lusaka and Livingstone, Zambia, July 28–August 2, 2002.

Munjeri, D. (1990a). Refocusing or Reorientation? The Exhibit or the Populace: Zimbabwe on the Threshold. In I. Karp and S. D. Lavine (eds). *Exhibiting Culture: The Poetics and Politics of Museum Display*. Washington, DC: Smithsonian Institution Press, pp. 444–456.

Murray, N. and Witz, L. (2014). *Hostels, Homes, Museum: Memorialising Migrant Labour Pasts in Lwandle, South Africa*. Cape Town: University of Cape Town Press.

Ndlovu, N. (2009). Decolonising the Mind-Set: South African Archaeology in a Postcolonial, Post-Apartheid Era. In P. R. Schmidt (ed). *Postcolonial Archaeologies in Africa.* Santa Fe, NM: School for Advanced Research Press, pp. 177–192.

Négri, V. (1995). *A Study of the Financial and Legal Autonomy of Museums in Africa*. Paris: ICOM.

Oberhofer, M. (2018). Conservation and Restoration as a Challenge for Museum Cooperation: The Case of the Palace Museum in Foumban, Cameroon. In T. Laely, M. Meyer and S. Ra (eds). *Museum Cooperation between Africa and Europe. A New Field for Museum Studies.* Kampala: Fountain Publishers/ Bielefield, Transcript Verlag, pp. 195–214.

Onciul, B. (2015). *Museums, Heritage and Indigenous Voice: Decolonising Engagement*. London: Routledge.

Onciul, B. (2019). Community Engagement, Indigenous Heritage and the Complex Figure of the Curator: Foe, Facilitator, Friend or Forsaken. In P. Schorch, C. McCarthy and E. Durr (eds). Manchester: Manchester University Press, pp. 159–175.

Onciul, B., Stefano, M. L., Hawke, S., Stone, P.G., Davis, P., Whitehead, C. (2017). *Engaging Heritage, Engaging Communities*. Boydell Press.

Oyo, E. (1994). The Conventional Museum and the Quest for Relevance in Africa. *History in Africa* 21: 325–337.

Pastor, J. (2000). Redefining Museology: Museum Management Theory: Theorising Our Museums: A South African Context. *South African Museums Association Bulletin* 24 (1): 21–25.

Peers, L. and Brown, A. K. (2003). Introduction. In L. Peers and A. K. Brown (eds). *Museums and Source Communities*. London: Routledge, pp. 1–17.

Pratt, M. L. 1992. Arts of the Contact Zone. *Profession* 91: 33–4.

Rammapudi, T. (2004). Zebra on Wheels Programm. *ICOM Education* 18.

Rasool, C. (2015). Human Remains, the Disciplines of the Dead, and the South African Memorial. In D. R. Peterson, Gavua, K. and Rassool, C. (eds). *The Politics of Heritage in Africa Economies, Histories, and Infrastructures*. Cambridge: Cambridge University Press, pp. 133–156.

Said, E. W. (1985). *Orientalism*, New Edition. Harmondsworth: Penguin books.

Sandahl, J. (2019). Addressing Societal Responsibilities through Core Museum Functions and Methods: The Museum Definition, Prospects and Potentials. *Museum International* 71 (281–282): 1–2.

Sandell, R. (2002). Museums and the Combating of Social Inequality: Roles, Responsibilities, Resistance. In R. Sandell (ed). *Museums, Society, Inequality*. London: Routledge, pp. 3–23.

Schmidt, P. R. (2009). What Is Postcolonial About Archaeologies in Africa? In P. R. Schmidt (ed). *Postcolonial Archaeologies in Africa.* Santa Fe, NM: School for Advanced Research Press, pp. 1–20.

Sealy, J. (2003). Managing Collections of Human Remains in South African Museums and Universities: Ethical Policy-Making and Scientific Value: Reviews of Current Issues and Research Findings: Human Origins Research in South Africa. *South African Journal of Science* 99 (5 & 6): 238.

Segobye, A. K. (2009). Between Indigene and Citizen: Locating the Politics of the Past in Postcolonial Southern Africa. In P. R. Schmidt (ed). *Postcolonial Archaeologies in Africa.* Santa Fe, NM: School for Advanced Research Press, pp. 163–176.

Shelton, A. (2013). *Critical Museology: A Manifesto. Museum Worlds: Advances in Research* 1: 7–23.

Silverman, L. H. (2010). *The Social Work of Museums*. London: Routledge.

Stam, C. (1993). The Informed Muse: The Implications of 'the New Museology' for Museum Practice. *Museum Management and Curatorship* 12 (3–3): 267–283.

Stanley, N. (2008). Introduction: Indigeneity and Museum Practice in Southwest Pacific. In N. Stanley (ed). *The Future of Indigenous Museums: Perspectives from the Southwest Pacific*. New York: Berghahn Books, pp. 1–22.

Taruvinga, P. and Ndoro, W. (2003). The Vandalism of the Domboshava Rock Painting Site. Zimbabwe: Some Reflections on Approaches to Heritage Management. *Conservation and Management of Archaeological Sites* 6 (1–1): 3–10.

Tindi, M. (2012). Museum, Peacemaking and Conflict Resolution. Paper presented at the *ICME-ICOM Annual Meeting*, Windhoek, Namibia, September 12–14, 2012.

Ucko, P. J. (1981). Report on a proposal to initiate 'Culture Houses' in Zimbabwe. Unpublished Report to the Government of Zimbabwe. Zimbabwe: Government Printers.

Ucko, P. J. (1994). Museums and Sites: Cultures of the Past within Education-Zimbabwe, Some Ten Years On. In Stone, P. G. and L. Molyneaux (eds). *The Presented Past: Heritage Museums and Education*. London: Routledge, pp. 237–272.

Vawda, S. (2019). Museums and the Epistemology of Injustice: From Colonialism to Decoloniality. *Museum International* 71 (281–282): 72–79.

Verges, Francoise. (2014). "A museum without objects." In: *The Postcolonial Museum: The Arts of Memory and the Pressures of History*, edited by I. Chambers, A. De Angelis et.al., 25–38. Burlington: Ashgate Publishing Company.

Vergo, P. (ed). (1989). *The New Museology*. London: Reaktion Books.

Wajid, S. and Minott, R. (2019). Detoxing and Decolonising Museums. In R. Janes and R. Sandell (eds). London: Routledge, pp. 25–35.

Watson, S. 2007. Museums and Their Communities. In S. Watson (ed). *Museums and Their Communities*. London: Routledge.

Weil, S. (2003). Beyond Big and Awesome: Outcome-Based Evaluation. *Museum News* 40–45: 52–53.

Witcomb, A. (2007). A Place for All of Us? Museums and Communities. In S. Watson (ed). *Museums and Their Communities*. London: Routledge.

Witcomb, A. and Message, K. (eds). (2015). *Museum Theory*. Hoboken, NJ: Wiley-Blackwell.

1 Beating the drums

Co-curatorship and the reconfiguration of colonial ethnographic collections

Introduction

Although Peter Vergo's (1989) concept of new museology was developed thirty years ago, the pace of change in museums in Africa has been slow and "new" practices are still being adopted. For our work, the idea of a "new museology" (Vergo 1989) is as crucial as it is a discourse around the social and political roles of museums that encourage new communication and new styles of expression in contrast to classic, collections-centred museum models. Vergo's ideas gave us a framework which allowed us to collaborate with communities, and this in turn informed how the drums were reorganized and subsequently presented in the museum. We adopted co-curation as a methodology which was underwritten by collaborations, shared authority and dialogue with the local community (Forster and Bose 2019; Macdonald and Morgan 2019; Mallon 2019; Schorch, McCarthy and Durr 2019; Thomas 2019.)

In the project, the first author, Njabulo Chipangura together with a team of other museum professionals, used collaborations and co-curation as methodologies that gave the community an equal voice in the process of reorganizing the drums. In light of this, Golding and Modest (2019: 94) argue that co-curatorship entails "taking an interest not only in objects as things but also in the people, changing practices and belief systems that lend them meaning." Thus, in our project, through curatorial collaboration with locals, the spiritual dimensions of the drums were focused on just as much as their physical and material aspects. As a result of this participatory approach and use of interactive Information Communication Technologies a new interactive exhibition was born in which drums were juxtaposed with video recordings showing how they were used by communities in real time. Visitors can now select videos of various traditional dances and music performed in different parts of Eastern Zimbabwe. By embracing this multi-vocal and innovative curatorial approach through a new display of traditional drums, Mutare Museum managed to challenge and unsettle museological practices that treated important cultural relics as static, mute materials removed from their cultural settings. In terms of museological practice, this exhibition also points to the need for a new museology in Africa, one that embraces communities as respected knowledge bearers. Most importantly, this demands a deep respect for local knowledge that was so disparaged in colonial times. In the contemporary societies, through co-curation projects, local communities become producers of knowledge rather than powerless objects of study or sources of information. They become active players in curatorial practices and participate in processes of self-representation.

Colonial classifications and misrepresentations in the old Beit Gallery

Mutare Museum has five permanent display galleries: Eastern Districts, Mezzanine, Transport, Boultbee and Beit. The Eastern Districts Gallery depicts flora of the region with an emphasis on natural spectacles such as the Chirinda forest in Chimanimani, the Save River and the Nyangani Mountain. All these landscapes are presented in their presumably pristine status with no mention of indigenous communities whose cultures for many years left a fingerprint. Similarly, the Mezzanine Gallery specifically looks at displays of wild animals that are found in Eastern Zimbabwe with an elaborate representation of taxidermized and stuffed species such as the African python, hyena, leopard, pangolin and a bushbuck. The Boultbee Gallery is named in memory of Captain E. F. Boultbee, who was one of the first curators of the museum. The firearms collection in this gallery was personally donated by Captain Boultbee and comprises various types of European-made guns and pistols. The Transport Gallery comprises a vintage car collection with European or American origin. These cars were donated to the museum by white settlers during the colonial period. The Beit Gallery, named after Sir Alfred Beit, a British philanthropist who died in 1906, encapsulates the values of the early Rhodesian museums, which served the interests of the white settler minorities. Of note is how this proprietor's link and association with the museum has survived to the present, so much so that the Beit Trust, established in honour of Alfred Beit in 2015, gave the museum a grant to conduct research which led to the reorganization of ethnographic objects at Mutare Museum, part of whose gallery was

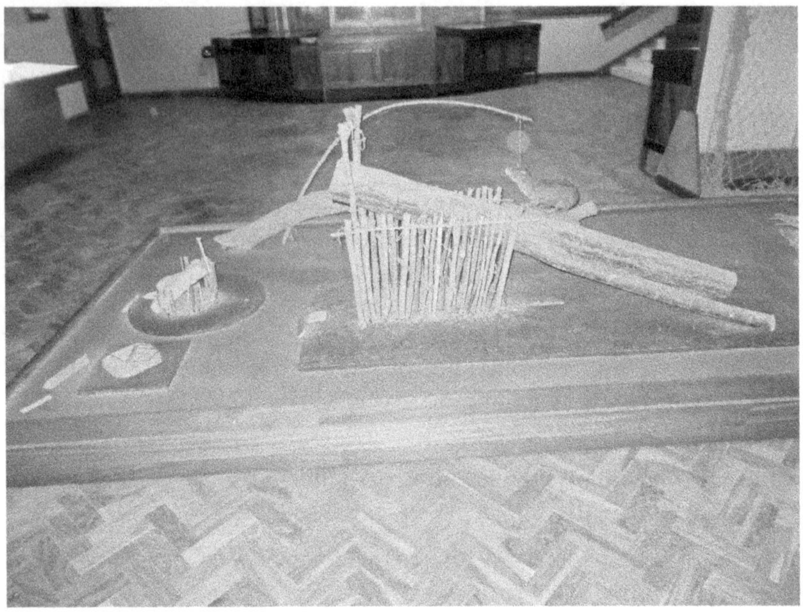

Figure 1.1 Old ethnographic exhibitions in Mutare Museum. Photograph by Njabulo Chipangura.

established in his memory. The trust gives developmental funding to Zimbabwe, Malawi and Zambia (the former Federation countries).

The gallery contains a wide range of exhibitions that covers themes related to the traditional aspects of the Shona[1] culture in Zimbabwe. The Alfred Beit Gallery in its old format before it was reorganized in 2016 comprised transport accessories in a glass case on the immediate left side of the entrance. Opposite this display were zoological displays comprising an animal tree and two cases with different kinds of insects (see Figure 1.1). Next to this was a display of traditional beehives containing live bees. Along the length of the gallery, there were a variety of mixed objects including geological displays and different types of traditional objects. Close to these was a display case with beads, head rests, snuffboxes and a portrait of a traditional chief adorned with symbols of chieftainship, such as badges and ceremonial artefacts. In this old set-up, displays in the Beit Gallery did not represent any coherent or meaningful story. Indeed, one could easily think this was a storeroom because the gallery had a mixture of a lot of different types of exhibits with no clear-cut theme or storyline. Thus, ethnographic objects were exhibited in a manner that conformed to the traditional practice of presenting objects exclusively for visual observation. This type of exhibiting did not do justice to the social biography of the collection, which cannot be understood in terms of a single unchanging identity, but rather by tracing the succession of meanings attached to the objects as they move through space and time (Edwards, Gosden and Phillips 2006). The problem was worsened by an improper presentation of the objects, which were dumped on the floor, displayed as strange, exotic and devoid of any social and historical significance to the way of life of the people (see Figure 1.1). In many cases, just like at Mutare Museum, colonial exhibitions often removed human history from material culture on display by presenting objects as cold and lifeless and disregarding their meaning and purpose which are intimately tied to human stories (Catlin-Legutko 2019: 41). During the reorganization of the old Beit Gallery we were conscious of the fact that objects connect people, places and events and also represent histories of continuity and change (Mallon 2019).

For many decades, the Mutare Museum had not reorganized the "misrepresented" ethnographic exhibits, curated before the end of colonial rule. In light of this, in 2014, more than three decades after Zimbabwe's political independence, the Mutare Museum curatorial team wanted to highlight and tell richer stories following the end of colonial rule. For starters, the gallery, named after Alfred Beit,[2] itself pointed to the colonial origins of the institution and the role that such exhibitions played during the colonial period – one of collecting and displaying the local environment and culture for the information and amusement of a small white settler community. For example, Shona traditional drums were only acquired during the colonial period as part of a broader trajectory in the scientific study of cultures of the "other." A display of these drums in the old Beit Gallery was premised on the idea of exoticizing cultures of the "other" by the colonial authority. However, this was done at the expense of their spiritual and everyday use. These objects were used for various rituals before they were dislocated from their original context and subsequently placed in the museum, and most of the rituals continue to be observed by local communities. As we were carrying out research for the new exhibition, we observed contemporary rituals in which the drums are still being used and are treated as living objects, cementing the project team's idea that the drums in the museum display could not continue to be disconnected from the past, but were to be seen and treated as enduring symbols that connect the past with the present and future (McCarthy, Hakiwai and Schorch 2019). This view is in contrast with how colonial ethnographers collected musical drums which were later displayed in the old Beit Gallery without an appreciation of where they came from and their original uses. During the colonial period, museum curators were endowed with authority in configuring ethnographic objects, thereby marginalizing local knowledge systems.

Being cognizant of their histories and connection to colonial forms of representing the "other," a question that always hounds museums that is connected with thousands of collections retrieved from local communities during the colonial era is what to do with these cultural treasures in the contemporary era. Collected by missionaries, white settlers and partly by museum personnel, deposited in museum store-rooms and displayed in museums that were patronized by only a small section of the community, these relics call for re-curation and reinterpretation to reconnect them with their true cultural meanings and contexts. Thus, in the decolonial turn, the museum curator – the expert – can no longer be a lone voice of authority but rather a facilitator of community engagement and collaboration (McCarthy, Hakiwai and Schorch 2019; Onciul 2019; Sandahl 2019). This can only work through collaborations, and in many cases, as in ours, these have transformed ethnographic museums from being places that were once regarded as displaying "others" to locations of cultural revitalisation, community voice and empowerment (Onciul 2019: 160). In our experience, co-curated projects have to be developed through collaboration between a museum and members of one or more communities, in a space where the authorities and voices are treated as equally as possible. It can, however, be argued that in such a setup the power dynamics are still asymmetric and skewed towards the institution – the museum – rather than the community. Yet in our experience, in all the engagements, the communities considered themselves to be the higher voice, the purveyors of their own culture and holders of knowledge that the museum sought.

Co-curation and the social biography of objects

We have in the ensuing chapter decried the almost obvious aspect that the development of museums in Africa coincided with the spread of colonialism and imperialism, and became part of a system that validated and justified oppression, dispossession and racial prejudice, where the study, collection and presentation of local cultures were seen as key aspects of exerting power and control over locals (Foucault 1998; Dubow 2006; Lord 2006). While acknowledging the contexts within which ethnographic collections were accumulated into the museum during the colonial period, we argue for looking beyond this tainted history to highlight how objects from this museum can indeed emerge in the postcolonial context, challenging inherited processes of confinement, classification and nomenclature entrenched by colonial museum practices. As argued by Mataga (2018), ethnographic objects have the potential to be retrieved from museums storehouses and thrust into the public sphere, allowing communities previously excluded from the museum space to enter the museum and influence curatorial activities (Mataga 2018). For this museum it was through co-curation and the development of collaborative exhibitions that museums are beginning to challenge the same ideas that they have been known to champion in the past. In doing so, museums are taking a leading role in decolonising, revisualizing, presenting alternative stories, interrogating intolerance and stimulating critical public pedagogies (Clover 2015). Though such activities, indigenous epistemologies and ontologies have also reshaped collecting and exhibiting practices in museums (Chipangura and Chipangura 2020). Co-curating as a methodology prioritises social history and the collecting of contemporary cultures in a dialogue with the community (Schorch, McCarthy and Durr 2019). Furthermore, in many post-colonial nations, sharing power with indigenous communities in the making of museum exhibitions is a methodology that is being used to pluralise, democratise and decolonize relations (Onciul 2015). Co-curation gives community members an equal voice in all aspects of exhibition development and results in a high level of participation (Ariese-Vandemeulebroucke 2018).

For many commentators, the ability of decolonial museology to engender a level of self-representation is a necessity, where previously marginalised knowledge can challenge colonially derived curatorial practices and reconnect objects with communities from where they were accumulated (Mignolo 2011). Most objects housed in African museums have strong spiritual significance, and new approaches of allowing communities to reconnect through using them can reframe museum practice (Mataga 2018). Furthermore, in Africa objects cannot be separated from the religious ceremonies with which they are associated (Konare 1995). If anything, the physical form of the object is considered to be a secondary element to its social and ritual structure (Arero 2005). Hence, it can be argued that in an African context objects are regarded as parts of an interconnected whole, and the superficial binary division between tangible and intangible does not exist. Although these objects may appear mundane with Western classifications, they carry with them important meanings connected to their ritual and cultural function within their societies of origin (Arero 2005: 21).

It is also important to note that even in many cultures, objects are not kept or preserved for their own sake, rather they are part and parcel of the changing social-cultural systems and are always intricately connected to the everyday living – the material, economic and social well-being of society. Perhaps one of the reasons local communities become detached from museums in Africa is the very fact that the museum treats cultural objects as ends in themselves, where the material and aesthetic aspects of objects override the spiritual and cultural value. Yet for many local communities, objects are a means to something – spiritual, cultural or personal. Objects are meaningless to society without their cultural values. For instance, we have seen that to many indigenous people, beyond the material and aesthetic aspects, their interest is in using the collections to address contemporary social and cultural issues. In an African context, objects like drums have potency and are treated by indigenous people as living beings which they can touch, smell and taste (Arero and Kingdon 2005; Mataga 2018; De Palma 2019). They constitute a part of an interconnected whole and thus we argue that the superficial binary division between tangible and intangible does not exist (Chipangura 2018). Although these drums appeared mundane within ethnographic classifications, they each had individual biographies and carry with them important meanings connected to their ritual and cultural functions located in their societies of origin (Arero 2005; Verges 2014; Golding and Modest 2019; McCarthy, Hakiwai and Schorch 2019).

A substitution of the object-oriented approach in favour of a community-centred approach means that objects are set aside in favour of their makers and their stories (De Palma 2019). Moreover, there is a need to look beyond the visible material evidence of an individual object to appreciating its aesthetic appeal while also discovering the epistemological systems and regimes of value that gave the object its original significance (Arero and Kingdon 2005). A museum collection is considered within indigenous perspectives as a process instead of a product because the latter is of secondary importance to the process of creation (De Palma 2019). In other words, such objects can be regarded as depositories of working capital which aids the reformulation of a future cultural renaissance (Stanley 2008). For us, the remaking of the Beit Gallery was essentially premised on these notions. It was meant to transform the way the museum treated cultural objects – change the processes by which the values/meanings are ascribed – by mainstreaming the voice of local communities.

In doing this, we prioritized what we termed decolonizing methodologies. As articulated elsewhere, we believed that some of the key decolonizing methodologies should include "critical analysis of social and political relations, collaborative consultation and research design, reclamation of cultural landscapes and heritage sites, repatriation of human remains, co-curation of archaeological collections, and devising more culturally accurate museum representations" (Bruchac 2014: 2069). It can only be through participatory approaches (Simon 2009) where we could change the nature of museum exhibition production. In coming up with a new Beit Gallery, narratives from the community were used in the storyline with minimal curatorial intervention. Thus, indigenous worldviews and forms of knowledge were incorporated in researching and reorganizing the Beit Gallery exhibition. As a result, a shared authority emerged in which we collaboratively worked with the community in producing the content. Community members informed the ways in which narratives in the exhibition were subsequently presented. In this regard, it can be posited that museums, especially in Africa, are being challenged to give up on their authoritarian voice of control and allow communities to speak for themselves. Accepting source communities as experts and research partners can change the museum practice by opening up different ways of knowing and caring for the past (Onciul 2019). We subscribed to the argument that curatorship has to evolve from being a strict specialised connoisseurship of individuals to a public service that attends to problems in contemporary communities (Schorch, McCarthy and Durr 2019: 5).

As indicated in the preceding paragraphs, we took the stance that the object is simply a small trace whose meaning emerges from a landscape and its true meaning can be social, religious, musical or literary (McCarthy, Hakiwai and Schorch 2019). For us, while we appreciated the material presence of the drums in the museum, it was the acknowledgement and understanding of the biography of the object that was even more important, i.e., looking at the individualization of its life before entering the museum (Kingdon 2005; Mataga 2018). In our experience, the biography of objects collected into the museum was related to the living aspects, the intangible and social lives or values of the same objects that continued to exist within the local communities. There was a complex but almost linear relationship between what we had in the Beit Gallery and what objects existed within the Hwesa community, reiterating the idea that objects in most African museums have sociological value because they belong to living cultures and are venerated. The objects in the old Beit Gallery, classified as "ethnographic" by the museum's classification protocols, marginalized the cultural values of these objects and amputated the cultural cords that connected these objects with their living tradition – the persistent cultural practices that existed outside the museum. The challenge for us was to make the reconnection.

New museology, curatopia and everyday uses of Shona ritual drums

As articulated in the introduction to this chapter, the idea of a "new museology" (Vergo 1989) is a discourse around the social and political roles of museums that encourages new communication and new styles of expression in contrast to classic, collections-centred museum models. According to Watson (2007: 13) "if we understand 'old museology' to be characterised by an emphasis on the professional collection, documentation and interpretation of objects, then 'new museology' is community focused with emphasis on community needs." Thus, the relationship between communities and museums is amplified in new museology in which communities become equal partners as well as controlling agents (Message 2013). New museology questions the idea of museums as storehouses and deconstructs power relations between museums and communities (Stam 1993). This concept recognizes the social and political role of museums and does so by encompassing meaningful community collaborations in curatorial practices (McCall and Gray 2014). Museums are also taking on new roles as brokers of culture with a shift of focus from conservation of material culture towards becoming forums for negotiating knowledge. Within the formulations of new museology, museums are regarded as stewards of objects, keeping them on behalf of local communities rather than being sole voices of authority in displaying and interpreting those objects (Peers and Brown 2003).

However, while some curators are happy to allow communities to temporarily act as co-curators, some are critical about the way in which being an expert is portrayed in these activities and feel that their expertise is trivialized. Discussions on new museology have been recently extended to encompass the notion of curatopia. Schorch, McCarthy and Durr (2019) define curatopia as an imagined future for an ideal socially and politically engaged curatorial practice. They argue that "curatopia explores the ways in which the mutual, asymmetrical relations underpinning global, scientific entanglements of the past can be transformed into more reciprocal, symmetrical forms of cross-cultural curatorship in the present" (Schorch, McCarthy and

Durr 2019: 2). Thus, curatopia as a concept looks at an emerging active reciprocal relationship between indigenous communities and museums. In the same vein, acknowledges that whilst in the past museums were perceived as elitist institutions, today they are developing closer working relationships with communities whose cultures and concerns they interpret. These views can also be read in light of what Meskell (2009) describes as a cosmopolitan approach in which experts are collaborating and sharing knowledge of the past with communities.

Whereas the old museum was imagined as a building, the new museum incorporates community perceptions and is imagined as both a process and an experience. Elsewhere, the concept of the contact zone formulated by Clifford (2007) and Pratt (1991) has allowed museums to evolve beyond easily definable, geographical arenas of interaction into becoming places for dialogue and intercultural exchange that bring people in contact with each other and establish ongoing relations. According to Peers and Brown (2003: 5) "artefacts function as 'contact zones' – as sources of knowledge and as catalysts for new relationships – both within and between these communities." Museums as contact zones bring communities together that were formerly spatially and politically separated through colonialism. Much in the same way, at Mutare Museum there was a paradigm shift in that we discarded our colonial outlook and adopted a new museological practice through collaborating with the community in conservations that generated new meanings for traditional drums. This community was consulted from the onset and they determined the ways in which the drums were subsequently represented in the exhibition. The drums were regarded not just as inert objects but as living beings that connected the past and the present in continuous ongoing relationships. Before this, Mutare Museum had been exclusively detached from communities whose cultures are presented in exhibitions. Nonetheless we argue that objects collected during the colonial period were not created in a vacuum, because they represent the coming together of a multiplicity of factors and possess individual biographies (Kingdon 2005; Mataga 2018; Golding and Modest 2019).

Museums beating the drums: traditional music and dance

Through collaborating with communities, Mutare Museum was able to establish the connection between the various drums in the museum to their ritual of meanings and uses – aspects which were neither captured nor represented in the old Beit Gallery. Through mutual agreements with the local traditional leaders, we video-recorded

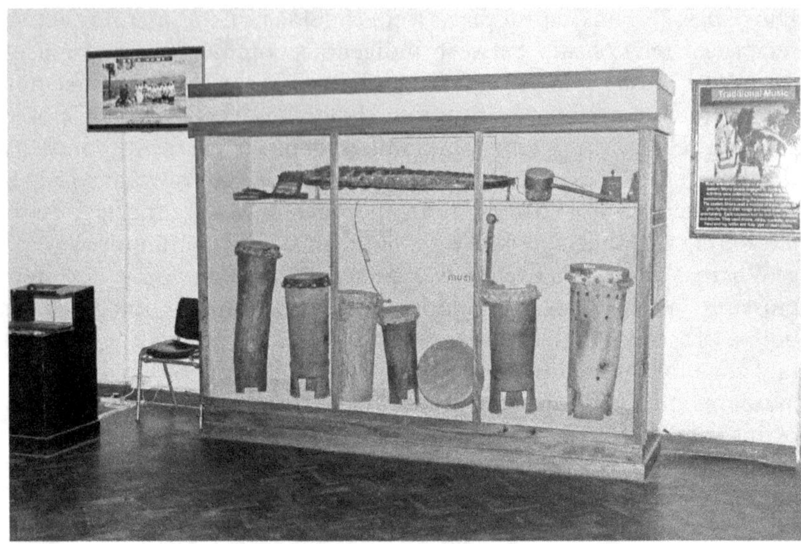

Figure 1.2 Traditional musical instruments display. Photograph by Njabulo Chipangura.

ritual ceremonies where the drums were being used and this helped to bring to fore alternative community epistemologies and ontologies which were absent in the old museum display. In these ceremonies it became clear that objects do not exist in isolation, but rather that they are intricately linked to other objects with ritual and ceremonial practices. For instance, we gathered that apart from drums, the community used several other instruments to give rhythm to their songs during the ritual ceremonies. They used *mbira* thumb pianos, *marimba*, *hosho*, hand and leg rattles and flute type instruments (see Figure 1.2). Each occasion had its own type of music, and we witnessed and video-recorded some of the dances during the research. Displayed in static glass cases, such connections are lost. The rituals described in the next section showed the futility of isolating individual objects and representing them in ways that do not acknowledge the complexity of their role in the cultural and spiritual practices of their original environments. Thus, in our case, one had to link the instruments and the dance (ritual, recreational or ceremonial).

In making attempts to link the instruments and the cultural context, the team was exposed to and recorded a number of dances. *Chimaisiri* is an example of a dance that we were given permission to record as it was performed by the community – punctuated by loud drumbeats. This dance was said to have been originally associated with hunting ritual ceremonies, but it is now also a social and recreational dance for beer parties, other joyful occasions and for funerals. For *Mhande*, another indigenous dance performed and accompanied by a drumbeat, within its ritual function, the *Mhande* repertoire consists of distinctive songs and rhythms used for communicating with the *Majukwa* (rain spirits). The rain spirits in turn communicate with God (*Mwari*) the provider of rain on behalf of the people. *Mhande* performance involves singing, drum beating, hand clapping, dancing and ululation. It was generally believed and accepted by this community that religion is a medium through which some complex problems of this earth, especially comprehension of life after death or life beyond the grave, can be addressed.[3] Against this background, we used collaborative co-curation in identifying similarities between drums used by the community during rituals and those found in our museum collection. The *Nhekwe* drums are cylindrical in shape, open and narrower at the bottom than the top. They were made from hardwood and top covered by animal skin secured on both sides with wooden pegs.

The other type of drum used was semicircular with a skin stretched over the opening and secured by wooden pegs. It was used during funerals, traditional ceremonies and festivities. By conducting this research, we aimed at bridging the gap between static objects displayed in the museum and similar objects that are being used in ceremonies. Co-curation also involved participant observation in these ritual ceremonies with a view of producing a comprehensive and empirically based reconstruction of past behaviours that informed us on the everyday uses of the drums displayed devoid of context at Mutare Museum. Thus, recognising that these drums were living and revered cultural objects embedded with spiritual and symbolic values enabled us to rethink old museological practices. As we were carrying out the research for this exhibition, we observed contemporary rituals in which drums are still being used and treated as living objects by Eastern Shona communities. In the process, we became facilitators of indigenous knowledge production in which the community was the central source of expertise. This collaborative approach to exhibition production is reflective of shared authority between the community and museum curators. Exhibitions have become more than just sites for the manifestation of preconceived curatorial theory as they increasingly turn into sites of collaborative research and knowledge production (Butler and Lehrer 2016). They have shifted from the status of merely presenting concluded results into important active venues for analysing social issues and producing relevant knowledge (Dahre 2019; Hansen, Henningsen and Gregersen 2019). Therefore, from the outset we collaborated with the community whose indigenous ritual ontologies determined the ways in which the drums were to be presented in the exhibition. We video-recorded ritual ceremonies where the drums were being used, and this helped to bring to the fore alternative community epistemologies and ontologies which were absent in the old museum display. We gathered that apart from drums, the community also used several other instruments to give rhythm to their songs during ritual ceremonies.

Making new connections: the new Beit Gallery interactive exhibition

In June 2016, the new Beit Gallery exhibition that emerged from this collaborative research was opened at Mutare Museum. This exhibition was the first wholesome post-colonial display at this museum designed with the full participation of the community through collaborations outlined above. The exhibition uses both audio and video depictions to illustrate the socio-cultural uses of the drums. In this exhibition, biographies of the drums connected to their various ritual uses are illustrated. Video recordings of ritual activities undertaken by the community using the drums are now a part of the storyline. Hence, new meanings absent in the old display emerged by linking the drums on display to their everyday use in their communities of origin. In the new Beit Gallery display, traditional drums no longer reflexively mirror cultures of the "other", instead they are playing an important role in the construction of social relations and new meanings located within community epistemologies and ontologies. These drums were once regarded as passive and inert objects that served colonial systems of classifications and the ethnographic gaze. Our strategy for reconnecting the drums in the museum with their lived traditions was to use interactive technologies. The new interactive exhibition depicts indigenous traditional music and musical instruments that are used during a variety of ritual and leisure time performances by the Eastern Shona people. Visitors to the museum also now have a high degree of association with musical instruments both on display and on the LED screens (see Figure 1.3). Within this set-up, visitors are able to see how the drums are used in Shona traditional ceremonies on video recordings (Chiwara and Chipangura 2019). Instead of thinking of ethnographic objects as possessing an unproblematic visual

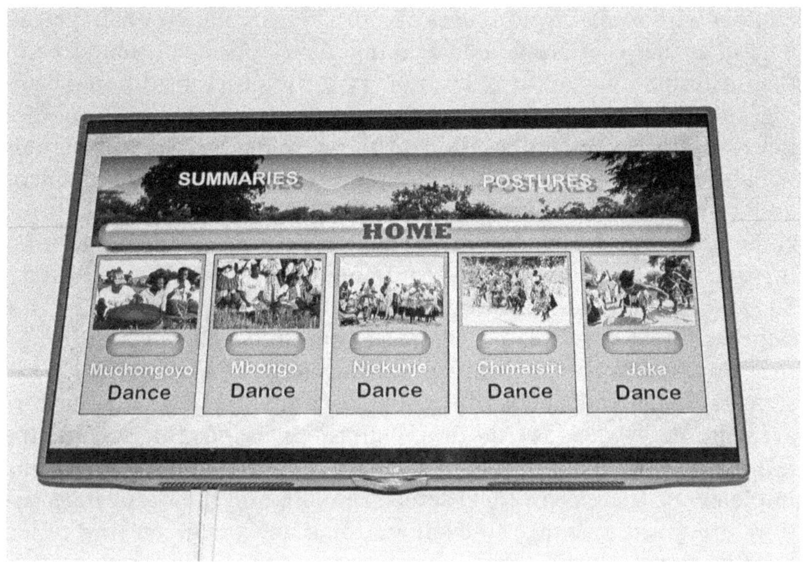

Figure 1.3 New Beit Gallery exhibition. Photograph by Njabulo Chipangura.

expressions – the exhibition in the reorganized Beit Gallery allows for multisensory interactions.

Our project thus integrated participatory knowledge production with digital technologies. We also considered the applicability of new museology and co-curation in the digital age by arguing that museums are no longer working for their community but with their community, where there is a participatory culture in which technology facilitates user-generated content (Bautista 2013). During the process of reorganising the Beit Gallery, new museum practices were embraced in order to encourage new ways of communication and expression absent in static collection based models where the focus was object conservation with no room for interactivity. The old Beit Gallery was fundamentally set out in such a way that the curator was the sole expert central to the museum practice. This also paved the way for transforming communities from being passive recipients of curatorial narratives into active agents in the production of exhibition narratives.

In the new exhibition, traditional drums are also displayed in combination with a series of high-resolution photographs and short traditional video dances, which all add up to the aura of the history of the Eastern Shona people. The new gallery also brings visitors into contact with socio-cultural uses of musical instruments on display in a manner that is exciting and engaging. An elaborate presentation of the Eastern Shona cultures, cosmology, agriculture, traditional healing, religious practices, music and community ontologies is another interesting interactive inclusion in the new Beit Gallery. Religious beliefs of Eastern Shona people are represented with the aid of videos and audio sounds of cultural songs associated with rain petitioning ceremonies. Also included in the new gallery is the theme of hunting and gathering that was a common feature among the Eastern Shona community since pre-colonial times. A reproduction of the hunting forest was created where visitors make their way through the immersive set of environments as they journey back in time to the sights, sounds and smells of the forest. In this small jungle, visitors are exposed to various traditional hunting methods that include the falling log trap and hunting nets. Apart from the jungle and hunting implements, there is an LCD screen mounted on the wall where visitors are given a chance to evaluate their knowledge on traditional hunting and gathering through a quiz session in the form of a flip book.

Conclusion

Museums need creative approaches to working with communities, in reinterpreting and giving new meanings to the ethnographic objects collected into museums during the colonial era, sometimes unethically. This chapter has presented strategies of how to deal with colonial objects (musical instruments) inherited from colonial museum practices that treated knowledge production in narrow ways that marginalized local knowledge and cultural practices while silencing the role of local communities in the museum curatorial practices. The display of musical instruments in unstructured, static ethnographic exhibits did a disservice to the objects and to the communities from which they were acquired. However, in the postcolonial era, with the advantage of digital technologies and changing frameworks/strategies of engagement with local communities, we can re-interpret objects and accord them more complex and holistic meanings that go beyond their material aspects to bringing out their cultural, religious and spiritual connections – aspects that are still persistent in the everyday lives of local communities. In many contexts the advantage is that beyond the calls for repatriation of material objects, local communities are eager and willing to be invited into the museum, work with the museum and contribute to the rectification of how their cultures and practices are represented in the museum. The next chapter extends this argument, showing how in another project in the museum, working with communities on a topical social issue, the museum can collaboratively work with communities in addressing social issues, using the museum as a site for social activism.

Notes

1 "Shona" is the name widely given to the largest linguistic and cultural group in Zimbabwe and is constituted by people who speak one similar language, also called Shona. However, the Shona language itself is not homogenous because within it are different dialects that vary from region to region. Eastern Zimbabwe is constituted by the Manyika, Ndau, Jindwi, Hwesa and Karanga speaking people. In this book we use Shona as a generic umbrella term for all different Shona speaking dialects as spoken in the communities found in Eastern Zimbabwe.

2 Alfred Beit (15 February 1853 – 16 July 1906) was a British gold and diamond magnate in South Africa and a major donor and profiteer of infrastructure development on the African continent. He also donated a great deal of money to university education and research in several countries and was the "silent partner" who structured the capital flight from post-Boer War South Africa to Rhodesia, and the Rhodes Scholarship, named after his employee, Cecil Rhodes.

3 Their whole social structure rests on religious beliefs and that of *Nyadenga/ musikavanhu* (God), the spiritual deity who is responsible for everyone's destiny. Since God was said to be in the spiritual world, He was not accessed by an ordinary human being, but through spirit mediums – *midzimu* – which can be family, clan or territorial levels. Thus, the community believes that when a person dies their spirit wanders about until it is given permission to come back and protect its children. Ceremonies are held which give these wandering spirits permission to come back. Only a fully grown person who has children can become an effective spirit medium. These ancestral spirits are believed to play a central role in the welfare of descendants and help and guide the families in their day-to-day lives. The spirits of the dead are believed to convey any message from the living to God and as such are central to the religion and belief of the community.

Bibliography

Arero, H. 2005. Tracing Contours of Creativity in Pastoralist Visual Culture. In H. Arero and Z. Kingdon (eds). *East African Contours: Reviewing Creativity and Visual Arts*. London: The Horniman Museum and Gardens, pp. 21–40.

Arero, H. and Kingdon, Z. (eds). 2015. Introduction: Visual Culture and Creativity in Eastern Africa: Reviewing a Neglected Branch of the Discipline. In *East African Contours: Reviewing Creativity and Visual Arts*. London: The Horniman Museum and Gardens, pp 1–5.

Ariese-Vandemeulebroucke, C. (2018). *The Social Museum in the Caribbean: Grassroots Heritage Initiatives and Community Engagement*. Leiden, The Netherlands: Sidestone Press.

Bautista, S. S. (2013). *Museums in the Digital Age: Changing Meanings of Places, Community, and Culture*. New York, NY: AltaMira Press.

Bennett, T. (1995). *The Birth of the Museum: History, Theory, Politics*. New York, NY: Routledge.

Bruchac, M. (2014). Decolonization in Archaeological Theory. In C. Smith (ed). New York, NY: Springer, pp. 20692077.

Butler, S. and Lehrer, E. (2016). Introduction: Curatorial Dreaming. In S. R. Butler and E. Lehrer (eds). *Curatorial Dreams*. London: McGill-Queen's University Press, pp. 3–26.

Catlin-Legutko, C. (2019). History That Promotes Understanding in a Diverse Society. In J. B. Cole and L. L. Lott (eds). *Diversity, Equity, Accessibility and Inclusion in Museums.* London: Rowman and Littlefield, pp. 41–48.

Chipangura, N. (2018). Cultural heritage Sites and Contemporary Uses; Finding a Balance between Monumentality and Intangibility in Eastern Zimbabwe. In C. Waelde et al., *Research Handbook on Contemporary Intangible Cultural Heritage Law and Heritage*. Cheltenham: Edward Elgar Publishing, pp. 379–398.

Chipangura, N and Chipangura, P. (2020). Community museums and rethinking the colonial frame of national museums in Zimbabwe. *Museum Management and Curatorship* 35 (1): 36–56.

Chiwara, D. and Chipangura, N. (2019). Digital Technology: The Panacea to Improve Visitor Experience, Audience Growth? *Museum International* 70 (1–2): 114–123.

Clifford, J. (2007). The Quai Branly in Process. *October* 120: 3–23.

Clover, D. E. (2015). Adult Education for Social and Environmental Change in Contemporary Pubic Art Galleries and Museums in Canada, Scotland and England. *International Journal of Lifelong Education* 34: 300–315.

Dahre, J. (2019). On the Way Out? The Current Transformation of Ethnographic Museums. In V. Golding and J. Walklate (eds). *Museums and Communities: Diversity, Dialogue and Collaborations in an Age of Migrations*. Cambridge: Cambridge Scholars Publishing, pp. 61–87.

De Palma, M. (2019). Selfies, Yoga and Hip Hop: Expanding the Roles of Museums. In V. Golding and J. Walklate (eds). *Museums and Communities: Diversity, Dialogue and Collaborations in an Age of Migrations*. Cambridge: Cambridge Scholars Publishing, pp. 230–259.

Dubow, S. (2006). *A Commonwealth of Knowledge: Science, Sensibility, and White South Africa, 1820-2000*. Oxford: Oxford University Press.

Durr, E. (eds). *Curatopia: Museums and the Future of Curatorship.* Manchester: Manchester University Press, pp. 90–106.

Edwards, E., Gosden, C. and Phillips, R. B. (2006). Introduction. In E. Edwards, C. Gosden and R. B. Phillips (eds). *Sensible Objects: Colonialism, Museums and Material Culture*. Oxford and New York: Berg, pp. 27–41.

Forster, L. and Bose, F. (2019). Concerning Curatorial Practice in Ethnological Museums: An Epistemology of Postcolonial Debate. In P. Schorch, C.

McCarthy and E. Durr (eds). *Curatopia: Museums and the Future of Curatorship.* Manchester: Manchester University Press, pp. 44–55.

Foucault, M. (1998). Different Spaces In R. Hurley (ed). *Essential Works of Foucault 1954–1984.* London: Penguin, pp. 175–185.

Golding, V. and Modest, W. (2019). Thinking and Working Through Differences: Remaking the Ethnographic Museum in the Global Contemporary. In P. Schorch, C. McCarthy and E.

Hansen, M. Henningsen, A., and Gregersen, A. (2019). Introduction. In M. V. Hansen, A. F. Henningsen and A. Gregersen (eds). *Curatorial Challenges: Interdisciplinary Perspectives on Contemporary Curating*. London: Routledge, pp. 1–6.

Kingdon, Z. (2005). Creative Frontiers: Sculptural Innovation and Social Transformation in East Africa. In H. Arero and Z. Kingdon (eds). *East African Contours: Reviewing Creativity and Visual Arts.* London: The Horniman Museum and Gardens, pp. 1–20.

Konare, A. (1995). The creation and Survival of Local Museums. In C. Daniel and E. Arinze (eds). *Museums and the Community in West Africa.* Washington, DC: Smithsonian Institution Press, pp. 5–10.

Lord, B. (2006). Foucault's Museum: Difference, Representation, and Genealogy. *Museum and Society* 4 (1–1): 11–14.

Macdonald, S. and Morgan, J. (2019). What Not to Collect? Post-Connoisseurial Dystopia and the Profusion of Things. In P. Schorch, C. McCarthy and E. Durr (eds). *Curatopia: Museums and the Future of Curatorship.* Manchester: Manchester University Press, pp. 29–43.

Mallon, S. (2019). *"He alo a he alo/kanohi kit e kanohi/* face to face: curatorial bodies, encounters and relations." In P. Schorch, C. McCarthy, and E. Durr (eds). *Curatopia: Museums and the Future of Curatorship.* Manchester: Manchester University Press, pp. 89–98.

Mataga, J. (2018). Museum Objects, Local Communities and Curatorial Shifts in African museums. In T. Laely, M. Meyer and R. Schwere (eds). *Museum Cooperation between Africa and Europe: A New Field for Museum Studies.* Kampala: Fountain Publishers, pp. 57–68.

McCall, V. and Gray, C. (2014). Museums and the 'New Museology': Theory, Practice and Organisational Change. *Museum Management and Curatorship* 29 (1–1): 19–35.

McCarthy, C., Hakiwai, A. and Schorch, P. (2019). The Figure of the Kaitiaki: Learning from Maori Curatorship Past and Present. In P. Schorch, C. McCarthy and E. Durr (eds). *Curatopia: Museums and the Future of Curatorship.* Manchester: Manchester University Press, pp. 211–226.

Meskell, L. (2009). Introduction. In L. Meskell (ed). *Cosmopolitan Archaeologies.* Durham, NC: Duke University Press, pp. 1–28.

Message, K. (2013). *Museums and Social Activism: Engaged Protests.* London: Routledge.

Mignolo, W. (2011). Museums in the Colonial Horizon of Modernity: Fred Wilson's Mining the Museum (1992). In J. Harris (ed). *Globalization and Contemporary Art.* Wiley-Blackwell, pp. 71–85.

Onciul, B. (2015). *Museums, Heritage and Indigenous Voice: Decolonising Engagement*. London: Routledge.

Onciul, B. (2019). Community Engagement, Indigenous Heritage and the Complex Figure of the Curator: Foe, Facilitator, Friend or Forsaken. In P. Schorch, C. McCarthy and E. Durr (eds). *Curatopia: Museums and the Future of Curatorship.* Manchester: Manchester University Press, pp. 159–175.

Peers, L. and Brown, A. K. (2003). Introduction. In L. Peers and A. K. Brown (eds). *Museums and Source Communities.* London: Routledge, pp. 1–17.

Pratt, M.L.M. L. (1991) Arts of the Contact Zone. *Profession* 91: 33–40.

Sandahl, J. (2019). Curating Across the Colonial Divides. In P. Schorch, C. McCarthy and E. Durr (eds). *Curatopia: Museums and the Future of Curatorship.* Manchester: Manchester University Press, pp. 72–89.

Schorch, P., McCarthy, C. and Durr, E. (2019). Introduction: Conceptualising Curatopia. In P. Schorch, C. McCarthy and E. Durr (eds). *Curatopia: Museums and the Future of Curatorship.* Manchester: Manchester University Press, pp. 1–16.

Simon, N. (2009). The Participatory Museum. Retrieved January 2, 2019 from http://www.participatorymuseum.org/read/

Stam, C. (1993). The Informed Muse: The Implications of 'the New Museology' for Museum Practice. *Museum Management and Curatorship* 12 (3–3): 267–283.

Stanley, N. (2008). Introduction: Indigeneity and Museum Practice in Southwest Pacific. In N. Stanley (ed). *The future of indigenous Museums: Perspectives from the Southwest Pacific*. New York: Berghahn Books, pp. 1–22.

Thomas, N. (2019). The Museum as Method (Revisited) In P. Schorch, C. McCarthy and E. Durr (eds). *Curatopia: Museums and the Future of Curatorship.* Manchester: Manchester University Press, pp. 17–119.

Vergo, P. (1989). Introduction. In P. Vergo (ed). *The New Museology* London: Reaktion Books Ltd., pp. 16.

Watson, S. (2007). Museums and Their Communities. In S. Watson (ed). *Museums and Their Communities*. London: Routledge, pp. 88–97.

2 Museum activism

Decolonised exhibition practices, public pedagogies and social change

Background and context: alluvial diamond mining in Chiadzwa

The discovery of surface diamonds in Chiadzwa, Marange[1] in around 2006 by members of that community set in motion a chain of events that led to their relocation to Arda Transau, Odzi by the government against their will. The alluvial diamond fields are in the municipal ward of Chiadzwa, about 80 miles southwest of the city of Mutare in the Manicaland Province of Zimbabwe. Between 2006 and 2007, this community, through many thousands of artisanal miners, was freely mining diamonds and was later joined by many other people from across the country as the government was yet to ascertain the real value of these precious stones (Chipangura 2019). Mining was carried out using basic rudimentary tools such as picks, chisels and shovels since the deposits were on the surface. However, in the middle of 2008 assay tests were carried out and the government moved in to restore order in the area by chasing away all the miners whom they considered to be illegal. During this period, with increasing militarisation of the diamond fields, plans were also put in place to relocate villagers (Gukurume and Nhodo 2020). Diamond mining then became an object of social inequality in Chiadzwa as local villagers were displaced to pave way for the establishment of formal diamond mining companies (Chipangura 2019). In spite of the fact that these mineral resources were touted to be some of the best diamond reserves in the world,[2] the discovery and exploitation of the minerals brought marginalisation for local communities. Instead of benefiting from the priceless value of the diamond, the villagers were further impoverished as a result of the displacement. Movement of the few villagers who remained in the area was severely curtailed with a curfew imposed under the watch of police and army details. Instead of improving the standards of living for the communities, the diamonds ended up benefiting a few elites and politicians and thus brought with it social exclusion. Villagers who were displaced by the advent of formal mining were relocated to Arda Transau, a government farm in Odzi located 75 km northwest of their original homesteads. Amid the rising contesting interests, the mining activities – particularly the involvement of the state in the activities – received worldwide condemnation of the minerals as "blood diamonds" (see Nyamunda and Mukwambo 2012). The state activities received criticism around human rights abuses and dispossession.

Museums, public pedagogies and social change

Exhibitions in museums are increasingly becoming popular public pedagogical strategies that engage with stories of social struggles faced by surrounding communities. As highlighted above, the case of the discovery of diamond mines turned into a story of displacement, repression and abuse of human rights for the local community. In responding to this social issue affecting communities in the vicinity of the museum, the museum adopted strategies of engagement that looked beyond its traditional mandate, thereby creating relationships with communities that reflected the museum as a site of foregrounding community-based challenges. Using its research, interpretive and public education tools/skills, the museum engaged in what we see as decolonial strategies – decolonial in the sense of transcending its traditional mandates of collection, classification and interpretation, to a process that foregrounded local stories and experiences. By looking at the research, design and the production of *Ngoda: The Wealth Beneath Our Feet* exhibition in the museum, we highlight how this strategy created a public forum for dialogue and in the process reframed the museum as a space for effecting social change. The discovery of surface diamonds in Chiadzwa, Eastern Zimbabwe in 2006 and the subsequent displacement of communities living in the area was a topical issue articulated in the exhibition for purposes of effecting social change.

Through this exhibition, the Mutare Museum (see Figure 2.1) provided a space where the community explored complicated conversations and controversies surrounding diamond mining. In view of the museum being an agent of social change, we use this exhibition to stimulate dialogue where ideas and engagement became more important than objects. This exhibition focused more on the people of Chiadzwa and their stories rather than objects, and the stories were

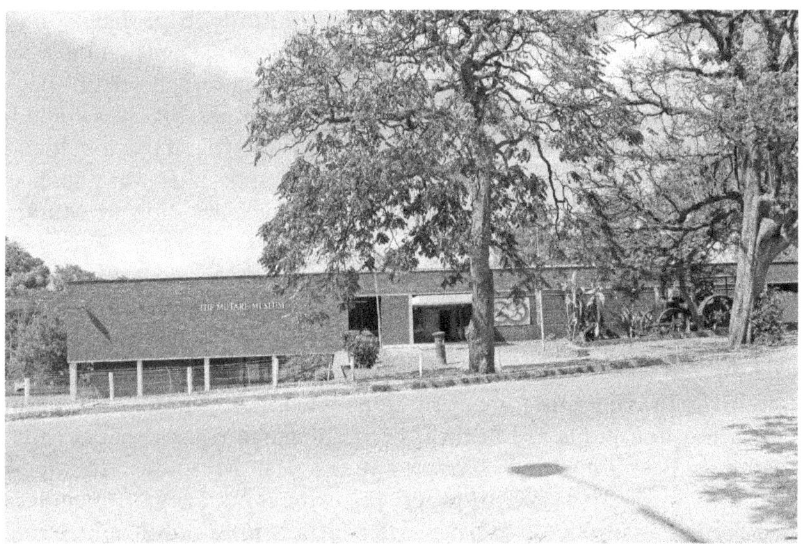

Figure 2.1 Showing the east-facing façade of the Mutare Museum. Photograph by Njabulo Chipangura.

presented as multifaceted and open for debate and interpretation. Methodologically, this exhibition was co-curated with members of the Chiadzwa community in order to bring out the aspect of multivocality. Quotes of community members were included in the design of the exhibition and their voices were embedded in every aspect, including in the narratives. Thus, we are going to look at the conceptualisation of this exhibition by Mutare Museum as a practice of public pedagogy as well as an agent for social change. This exhibition will be presented as part of a public pedagogical practice that engendered decoloniality at Mutare Museum. We also show how adult education in public museums through exhibitions has the ability to influence social change (Chipangura 2019). Exhibitions that address contemporary challenges can stimulate dialogue amongst affected communities and advance learning. Museums by nature are public pedagogical institutions with a host of adult education opportunities and have over time responded to the needs of local communities with regard to promoting social transformation using exhibitions (Clover et al. 2016). By being an important public pedagogical institution, Mutare Museum took an active role in addressing challenges faced by communities in Chiadzwa through a decolonial exhibition that was produced using collaborative and participatory approaches. Moreover, curating is a form of pedagogy which can propose solutions to problems, and exhibitions that are produced have been described as epistemological technologies of change (Hansen, Henningsen and Gregersen 2019).

A decolonised museum encompasses multiple perspectives embedded in values, norms and cultural practices that often tell difficult and troubling stories in its exhibitions (Vawda 2019). This was the case in point with the Chiadzwa diamond mining exhibition at Mutare Museum. This exhibition provided a decolonial space that addressed unjust mining practices. Most museums across the world, and particularly in Africa, have well-documented histories of elitism, exclusion and colonialism and subsequently have been left out from the debates and discourses of critical public education (Clover 2015). However, of late through contemporary exhibitions which are a practice of adult education, museums are beginning to challenge the same ideas that they have been known to champion in the past. Museums are important and productive sites for practicing critical pedagogies, including decolonizing practices, social movement learning, adult education, popular education and citizen education (Clover et al. 2016). Therefore, adult education practices through museum exhibitions can promote knowledge, democracy, imaginative thinking and an engaged citizenry with agency to shape their own learning and lives (Clover et al. 2016). As a public institution that promotes informal adult learning through community engagements, Mutare Museum also encourages dialogue and social inclusion.

By conceptualizing *Ngoda: The Wealth Beneath Our Feet* exhibition, this museum moved in to challenge contemporary social problems and provided a platform for dialogue and learning amongst members of the Chiadzwa community. Communities are valuable sources of expertise and partners in knowledge creation and not passive recipients of authorised discourses. They are no longer just people who enjoy museum products but are also actively directing the activities of museums and can choose exhibition themes (Golding, 2016). Thus, Butler and Lehrer (2016) argue that collaborative projects are becoming a key unit of knowledge production in the humanities. Hence in a museum, the collaborative production of exhibitions can also be reflective of shared authority between the community and museum practitioners. Elsewhere, as argued by Bell and Clover (2017: 27) museums can use "collaborative and participatory approaches that encourage society-wide reflection and dialogue and apply a uniquely aesthetic and historical lens to contemporary problems." In doing so museums have taken a leading role in decolonising, revisualising, presenting alternative stories, interrogating intolerance and stimulating critical thinking (Clover 2015). Similarly, today in many post-colonial nations sharing power with indigenous communities in the making of museum exhibitions is a methodology that is being used to pluralise, democratise and decolonize relations (e.g., Schmidt 2009; Onciul 2015). Participatory approaches, as argued by Simon (2009), also fundamentally change the nature of museum exhibition production. At Mutare Museum, we employed community engagement and collaboration as an adult education practice in researching and creating this exhibition. Such type of collaboration can be regarded as a decolonial strategy because during the interview process, we embraced community perspectives as they came out, and these were subsequently presented in the exhibition with minimal curatorial intervention. The use of collaborative approaches provided an opportunity for diverse co-produced stories in which members of the community learned some of their challenges from each other. By engaging people with each other in a dialogue during exhibitions, museums can become ideal sites for transformative educational practices (Przesmitzki and Grenier 2008).

Narratives from the community displaced by the setting up of formal diamond mines were collected using interviews and were used in the storyline with minimum curatorial intervention. As a result, a shared authority emerged in the process of making the exhibition with both curators and representatives of the affected community collaboratively working together on the content. The community agreed to share stories of their struggle and daily challenges that were used in production of the exhibition using video and audio descriptions. In essence, it can be argued that museum exhibitions can provide empowering learning experiences to the community by employing self-reflexive techniques of representation (Styles 2011). As a site of adult education, Mutare Museum allowed members of the Chiadzwa community to acquire skills and knowledge and capacity to think critically outside the traditional "classroom" learning spaces. Thus, in coming up with *Ngoda: The Wealth Beneath Our Feet* exhibition, power and authority was shifted from didactic curatorial authority towards active community participation, co-curatorship and co-interpretations that challenged existing conceptions of knowledge and knowing. Clover, Sanford and Johnson (2016: 2) argue that adult education is "…a space of encounter, a more democratic practice of collective critical and creative exploration and engagement." In both museums and galleries, adult education is undertaken through curated exhibitions and displays (Clover, Sanford and Johnson 2016). In our case the exhibition was collaboratively produced with the Chiadzwa community.

The process of making *Ngoda: The Wealth Beneath Our Feet* exhibition

Mutare Museum as a public pedagogical institution responded to the situation in Chiadzwa through conducting research that led to the production of an exhibition that positioned the concerns of the local community and at the same time advocated for social justice and transformation. This we did because we felt that a museum exhibition could challenge contemporary social problems that were being faced by the Chiadzwa community and at the same time give space for dialogue and conversations on how to provide solutions. Mutare Museum took up the contentious issue of diamond mining and displacements by engaging disfranchised villagers through interviewing them from February to May 2013. The research team that carried out the interviews and later the installation of the exhibition consisted of two curators, an exhibition designer, a technical officer and a marketing officer. Apart from the interviews, data used for making the diamond mining exhibition was obtained through the analysis of news sources. Since the discovery of surface diamonds in Chiadzwa in 2006, there were a lot of newspaper and TV reports on artisanal diamond mining activities by the community. A desktop study to understand the different reports on artisanal diamond mining in Chiadzwa was carried out mostly relying on *The Manica Post*, other newspapers and various news clips from the national broadcaster, Zimbabwe Television (ZTV).[3] A close analysis of these primary sources revealed the complexity of artisanal diamond mining and the different activities that were undertaken by the community before being displaced. These activities in their captured pictorial formats were used to develop part of the diamond mining exhibition's storyline.

The other methodological approach we used during the research was collecting mining tools which we included in the exhibition not as mute artefacts, but as objects that embodied and reflected certain ideas, knowledge and skills of mining by the villagers. In the exhibition we therefore integrated biographies of the tools using both pictorial and textual narratives. Tools collected for the exhibition included picks, shovels, chisels, carrying bags and hammers. Their biographies were documented by recording narratives about how they were procured, used and disposed of when the villagers were removed from Chiadzwa. Interviewed community members were able to give out detailed biographical information of how they used these tools and how they wanted the techno-social stories associated with them to be represented in the exhibition. To get detailed information on the contentious issue of relocations and the cultural destruction caused, interviews were carried out with the affected community members. It has also been argued that upon the attainment of political independence in Zimbabwe, the indigenous population expected an about-turn in the ways in which their ethnographic collections were being presented in museums. Debates focused on when they would be accorded respect, consultation, involvement and engagement in setting up museum displays. Thus, we framed and collaboratively designed the diamond exhibition with a view to giving the community a voice without too much of our curatorial intervention. In any case, we strived to balance curatorial formulations with community aspirations, thereby allowing the exhibition to reflect shared voices. We prioritized the idea of learning together and from each other by sharing the responsibility of developing this exhibition with the Chiadzwa community.

Using the shared voice approach, we interviewed villagers who were relocated from Chiadzwa by the government in paving way for the establishment of formal mines and allowed them to express their honest views, which were to be reflected in the exhibition. The stories of the villagers shared in the exhibition revealed the contentious nature of the relocations. People who had lived in the area for more than 70 years lost their homesteads, leaving behind their cultural heritage in the form of graves and other cultural practices that they had been accustomed to. Each family was given a core house with four rooms, and by the time of the exhibition 1000 families had been relocated. The issue of compensation also came out clearly and we were told about the money they were promised which at the time of researching for the exhibition had not been paid. This form of community engagement during the research shows that Mutare Museum became an active agent of social change and a site of critical adult learning and public pedagogy.

Public pedagogy has been defined as processes, types and sites of education and learning occurring outside formal education institutions (Borg and Mayo 2000; Grenier 2010; Burdick and Sandlin 2013). Museums are sites of cultural politics and public pedagogy that democratize production of knowledge by creating reflexive spaces for addressing topical issues in which curators work collaboratively with communities (Giroux 2011). At the same time, self-reflexive museum exhibitions allow curators to engage communities (Styles 2011). In this regard, it can be argued that adult education through this exhibition disrupted tendencies of social exclusion and marginalisation for which Mutare Museum used to be known during the colonial period. As part of the data collection phase for the exhibition, we also had the chance to observe the actual mining that was instituted by the government after relocation of the villagers. Thus, we were able to observe some of the technical operations at the established formal mines. Thereafter we produced a comprehensive pictorial record of the formal mining. Permission to photograph for this research was granted by the Ministry of Mine and Mineral Development which was the authority responsible for the mining and selling of the diamonds. These photographs were juxtaposed with the pictures of early community mining activities in the final exhibition at Mutare Museum. We did this in order to provoke debate and dialogue.

Having collected our data through interviews, observations, desktop surveys, pictures and collecting of mining objects, we mounted the exhibition on 5.5 × 4 feet upright boards; 5 inches in thickness, which featured text panels, images, and captions organized around the exhibition's themes (Chipangura and Marufu 2019). In addition to these, a multimedia display retold the stories of villagers who were relocated from the diamond field to Arda Transau Farm in Odzi. During the diamond mining exhibition, Mutare Museum became a site of adult learning where alternative information was shared about the social ills of mining and thereafter dialogue was initiated for social change. This exhibition became a space of critical public pedagogy which stimulated conversations in which the Chiadzwa community spoke about what was happening around them. For this reason, Grenier and Hafsteinsson (2016: 12) argue that "... museums can support and encourage radical thinking in action through public pedagogy and social movement learning in both the content they choose to highlight and their approaches to representation and engagement." Elsewhere, Banz (2015: 43) also argues that "museums promote autonomous individual learning and accommodate self-directed adults interested in pursuing their own education with a purpose in discovering immediate applications of learning." Museums allow adults to have a degree of autonomy as they learn from exhibits and displays.

Themes of the exhibition

The exhibition was divided into four thematic sections that chronicled the story.

In *Ngoda: The Wealth Beneath Our Feet – Community Mining Phase (2006–2008)*, photographs and maps laid out the historical background of Chiadzwa diamond fields and the discovery of surface diamonds by the community. This discovery evolved in a diamond rush.

By 2008, close to 10,000 people, mostly unemployed youths from across the entire country, had descended on the mining fields. This period was popularly known as *bvupfuwe* in local parlance, referring to the open and free mining for all without any restrictions by law enforcement agents (see Figure 2.3). "Ngoda" then became a buzzword used by community miners in referring to diamonds. It was derived from the word *ungoda chi-i*, a Shona phrase used by the traders to ask the miners what they preferred in exchange for the diamonds. At the time, because the miners were not aware of the true value of the diamonds, there was a barter trade in which they were exchanged for commodity items such as sugar, cooking oil, mealie meal and rice (Chipangura 2019; Chipangura and Marufu 2019).

In the second section, *Formal Diamond Mining in Chiadzwa (2009 to Present Day)*, text and images explored the start of a new era (see Figure 2.2). With the end of community mining the government moved in to establish formal mines to harness the diamonds. This panel depicted the formal mining technologies and essentially was designed to give the public an overview of the mining after the relocation of the community.

In the third section of the exhibition, we used multimedia to tell the stories of villagers who were relocated from their homestead to Arda

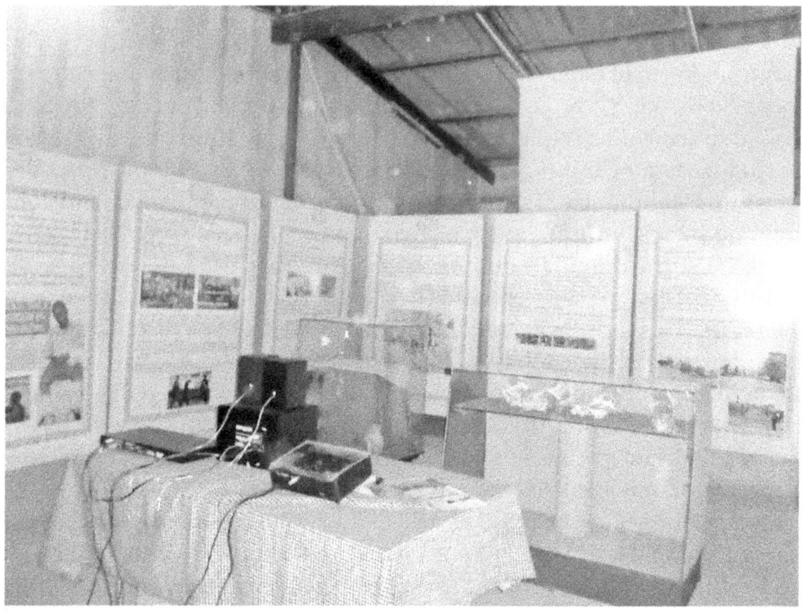

Figure 2.2 Second section. Photograph by Njabulo Chipangura.

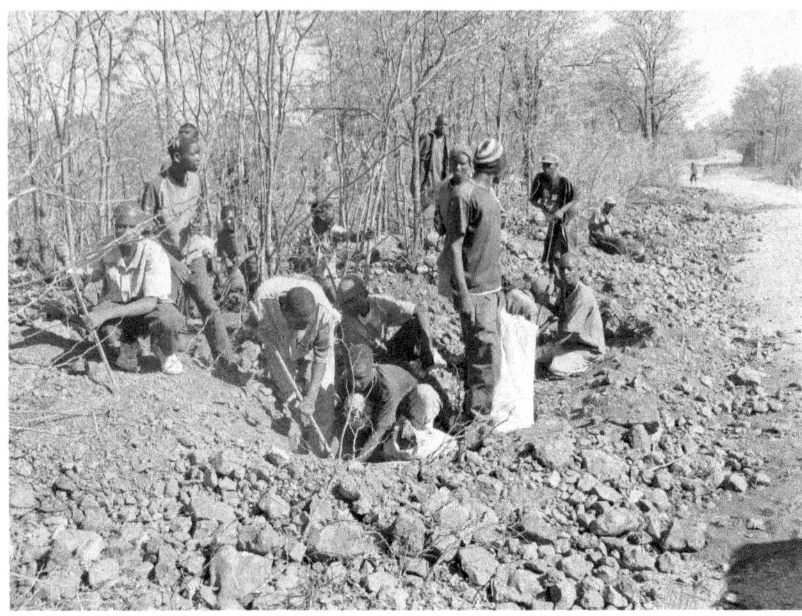

Figure 2.3 Some of the community miners during the diamond rush period. Photograph by *Manica Post*.

Transau Farm in Odzi. Audio and video narratives of the villagers were beamed through a projected wall display, to give the public a chance to relate to the whole sequence of events, from community mining to the formalization of mining and relocation of villagers. We purposefully used this technique to frame and reinforce identity and belief and convey the socio-cultural values of the villagers derived from their sense of place at the diamond mining area before they were moved to Arda Transau. A few graves were said to have been relocated to another cemetery, but this move was not enough, as villagers kept on complaining about graves of their relatives that they left behind in Chiadzwa. Loss of land became a major bone of contention amongst the villagers and this was portrayed in this section of the exhibition. In the videos, villagers also vented their dissatisfaction with the way in which the government had tackled relocations. A strong call was also sent out using video petitions for the government to allow the remaining villagers in Chiadzwa to move freely without police or military harassment.

In the fourth section, *Staying Put: Challenges Faced by the Remaining Villagers*, we presented challenges that are being faced by the remaining villagers who are yet to be relocated (Figure 2.2).

This section revealed that access to the area was difficult because it was heavily securitised, and as a result the villagers were not free to move in and out of the diamond mining field. The community was also presented in this section as still living in abject poverty because they were not benefitting anything from the formal diamond mining.

Exhibiting and addressing social issues: community conversations and dialogue

With the rolling out of this exhibition, Mutare Museum suddenly became a nerve centre of adult education with debates centring around the need to compensate Chiadzwa villagers. In this regard it can be argued that the museum promoted social change through exhibits and educational programmes that raise public awareness of social issues and encourage effective action (Silverman 2010). We hoped that Mutare Museum through its exhibitory strategies would have the potential to change people's attitudes, values, knowledge and behaviours regarding the challenges caused by mining in the area. Sharing power as we did in making this exhibition is one of the most important manifestations of the new museological praxis which incorporates source community needs and perspectives (Peers and Brown 2003). The exhibition created a platform for the communities to have their voices heard by the authorities. For instance, through this exhibition villagers advocated for the repealing of the decision to declare sections of Chiadzwa community as "protected areas" under the *Protected Places and Areas Act,* Chapter 11*:12*. The exhibition illustrated how this law resembled pre-independence laws that were designed to keep Africans confined and how this had brought untold suffering to the people of Chiadzwa. Because of this law they were no longer able to freely move in and out of Chiadzwa as they were constantly subjected to inhumane searches for diamonds, and when found without identification documents on them they were severely harassed by police and soldiers, who also become notorious for constantly setting vicious dogs on villagers, which in numerous instances resulted in deaths. Community members interviewed during the research also revealed that owing to the *Protected Areas Act*, relatives and friends of those living in Chiadzwa were no longer able to visit them when they needed to, even in the case of emergencies such as funerals. They were required to first go to the Ministry of Home Affairs to seek a permit to enter Chiadzwa – a rule that effectively makes it impossible for outsiders to get in. Another major concern raised by the villagers during this engagement was the growing level of poverty in spite of the fact that there is immense mineral wealth in Chiadzwa. In addition to the fact that not a single new school or a clinic has been built from the proceeds of diamond wealth, the roads that lead to the diamond fields are in an advanced state of dilapidation, making it hard for vehicles travelling to Chiadzwa to safely access the area. The damage to the roads had been worsened by the mining companies' huge trucks that were used to transport goods to and from the diamond mines. The villagers appealed to the mining companies and the government to put tar roads to improve their condition.

All these views shared by the villagers were presented in the exhibition's storyline, and this can be regarded as a strategy used by the museum to address social inequality. In undertaking this kind of an exhibition, it can be argued that Mutare Museum embraced what Karp and Kratz (2014: 282) refer to as the "interrogative museum … which purposefully moves away from exhibitions that seem to deliver a lecture [which] might be declarative, indicative, or even imperative in mood – to a more dialogue-based sense of asking a series of questions." By addressing contentious issues that surrounded the mining of diamonds and the losing of cultural and land rights by villagers who used to stay close to the mining fields, the exhibition generated interest amongst diverse stakeholders and, as a result, the issue of compensation began to gain public attention. Eventually, out of the outcry that emerged from this exhibition, the villagers were financially compensated by the government and the mining companies and the idea of Community Share Ownership Trusts (CSOTs) also emerged. Dialogue about compensation stimulated by this exhibition encouraged the government to consider establishing community trusts. As a result, the Marange–Chiadzwa CSOT was formed by the government, and the five mining companies each seeded 10,000 USD towards community development projects.

By formulating exhibitions that address socio-cultural challenges facing communities such as this one, museums can become active agents of social change. Once bastions of high culture which only kept objects for the public gaze, museums can instead become interactive platforms where social issues can be articulated, discussed and solved for the benefit of once-marginalised people (Chipangura 2019). Within this new vision undergirded by social activism and socially engaged activities that have a direct bearing on communities' aspirations, museums can be multi-vocal spaces. The museums' exhibitionary tools/approach can be efficiently mobilized to give space to marginalized voices and get their concerns heard and perhaps addressed by authorities.

The diamond mining exhibition stimulated and provoked dialogue amongst people living in and around Mutare, and by doing this the museum provided a platform for public education, which is an essential output of new museology. In new museology there is showcasing of "histories of non-elite social strata" whereby museums move away from elitist viewpoints by embracing interpretations that have a bearing on hot-spot community issues (Watson 2007). Thus, in a way this exhibition gave the Chiadzwa community a chance to voice their own grievances and daily struggles for recognition. Essentially, Mutare Museum redirected its attention to focus more on adult education whilst at the same time redefining its curatorial functions by collaboratively producing the exhibition working together with the Chiadzwa community. Against the background that Mutare Museum used to be regarded as a clear and irrefutable sender of messages, it can be posited that the diamond mining exhibition diverted from this stance by allowing for the inclusion of multiple voices and for the adoption of a social mission. Not only did the museum become an active site of adult education during this exhibition, it was also transformed into an arena of contemporary social interaction and dialogue. In part, the exhibition also grappled with other social issues such as the effects of high levels of unemployment in Zimbabwe which forced many people to join illegal mining, drug abuse by the miners, illicit smuggling of diamonds and the topical issue of relocating villagers without meaningful compensation. This exhibition also successfully allowed for an open dialogue between the community, the government and civic rights groups like the Centre for Natural Resources Governance – an NGO that has been fighting for the Chiadzwa community to be given mining rights and decent compensation following their relocation to Arda Transau.

On the official opening of this exhibition on 18 May 2013, Chiadzwa villagers again took the opportunity to share their grievances. Video and the audio recordings which recounted stories of relocations particularly aroused deep emotions. Although some villagers acknowledged that newly built houses at Arda farm were nice, they complained that there wasn't enough grazing space for their cattle because the partitioned pieces of land were relatively small as compared to what they previously owned in Chiadzwa. The then-governor of the province, Christopher Mushowe, who was the guest of honour at the opening ceremony, was challenged with a barrage of questions by villagers and in return promised that the government was going to process financial compensation for the villagers in a timely manner and as a matter of urgency.

The need to exhume and rebury human remains left in Chiadzwa diamond fields was also discussed in many video recordings. The guest of honour also took note of this concern and assured that the government would rebury the remains, which would come along with a financial compensation of $1000 USD per grave. It can thus be argued that this exhibition was able to project and address certain expectations of the community, as well as answer some of their burning questions. Furthermore, members of both the private and state media who witnessed the dialogue generated by the exhibition also took the story of compensation to the front pages of their publications. For instance, *The Daily News* of 28 May 2013 carried the headline "The Diamond Mining Exhibition opened at Mutare Museum." The article highlighted the need for people from all sectors in the country to reflect carefully on the exhibition and to pay attention to the complexities surrounding the mining of diamonds in Chiadzwa.

This exhibition also brought to light certain human rights abuses that came to be associated with the formalisation of diamond mining in Chiadzwa. Key abuses that were recorded through interviewing villagers included forced relocations, loss of land and cultural rights as well as persistent harassment at the hands of police and military officials. Thus, the diamond exhibition became a public pedagogy practice as well as being a powerful medium for challenging human rights abuses that the villagers were facing. The exhibition advocated for social change by supporting the need to formalize diamond mining for the benefit of the whole nation rather than individuals. Economic benefits that the country as a whole could accrue from the formalisation of the mining were also highlighted in the exhibition. Revenue generated from mining could potentially provide a perfect chance to stabilize the collapsing economy with an unemployment rate of around 95 percent. Questions about the illegality and legality of the diamond mining activities were also addressed in the exhibition. Chiadzwa villagers did not consider their mining activities as illegal. They claimed it was their ancestral land and hence they took it as their right to mine the diamonds. Thus *Ngoda: The Wealth Beneath Our Feet* exhibition sought to present the histories of a socially marginalised Chiadzwa community as far as having rights to mining diamonds in their ancestral home. Such type of socially purposeful museum exhibitions can support human rights of different communities whose lived experience of marginalization is often reflected in their exclusion or misrepresentation (Sandell 2017; Janes and Sandell 2019).

Museum activism: Mutare Museum as an agent of social change

Apart from the diamond mining exhibition, Mutare Museum had actively previously functioned as an agent of social change in several platforms in response to community expectations. In 1998 an HIV and AIDS temporary exhibition was launched with the aim of discouraging societal stigmatization towards those suffering from this disease. In April 2011, the museum hosted a witchcraft talk show with a moving testimony by a young girl who narrated how she was recruited into witchcraft-related activities against her will by elders in her community. By engaging with such topical issues bedevilling the society, the museum did not only transform into social space where culturally sensitive matters were discussed but also played a critical pedagogical role towards the counselling and rehabilitation of this traumatised young girl. As a means to this end, a team of psychologists, traditional healers and professionals in non-governmental organisations who attended the talk show as speakers offered counselling, financial and material help to the victim. The decision of hosting this talk show was arrived at after the museum had been inundated by inquiries from visitors who wanted to see "witchcraft snakes." Before the witchcraft talk show, the ordeal of the young girl had spread throughout the city and subsequently generated much interest, with false rumours circulating alleging that the snakes had been captured and were now kept in the museum. In an African set-up, keeping snakes (except by museums or National Parks) is mythically associated with witchcraft activities. Furthermore, the swelling rumour about witchcraft snakes seems to have been substantiated by the fact that our museum has a section with live snakes in one of the display cases.

Elsewhere, Mutare Museum also acted as an agent of social change in 2012 by initiating an ethnographic study that documented different stories from victims of road traffic accidents in the city which were subsequently presented in an exhibition. This in itself can be regarded as a platform that supported the museum's growing strength in social activism. Surviving victims of accidents were given a chance to share their experiences as part of their psychological healing and also as an educational strategy to mitigate road carnage. This exhibition acted as a pedagogical tool which highlighted the dangers associated with the following human behaviours: drinking and driving, speeding, use of road-unworthy vehicles, flouting road regulations, night driving and overloading. The timing of this exhibition was particularly important as it coincided with the festive season, a period that traditionally recorded the highest number of road carnages in the country. Moreover, since Mutare Museum is the designated national collector of transport and antiquities, the exhibition also allowed for further engagement between the public and vintage cars on display. Therefore, reimaging Mutare Museum as a site of activism brought with it a new capacity to bring about social change. Mutare Museum managed to act as an agent that promoted social change by using this exhibition as a methodology that went on to reduce road traffic accidents in the city. Overall, the key lesson that emerged out of this was the ability of an exhibition to stimulate dialogue that can have a positive change on contemporary social issues (Sandell 2007).

Lessons from Chiadzwa: new museology and community collaboration

In creating *Ngoda: The Wealth Beneath Our Feet* exhibition, working with information and stories from affected communities, we presented in detail the history of the discovery of diamonds in Chiadzwa, Marange, giving space to the narratives of locals.[4] The tale of Marange diamonds was told in this exhibition as a practice of adult education that revealed the period from which the surface diamonds were "discovered" by the community to their relocation to pave way for formal mining. While the main aim of the exhibition was to educate the public about the socio-economic significance/effects of the discovery of diamonds in Marange, it was giving space for local narratives of the experiences of displacement that made the exhibition be seen as relevant by the community. Thus, in the process of creating this exhibition we used the engagement zone as a critical adult education methodology that gave Chiadzwa villagers agency in shaping narratives which were presented in the exhibition. They described the challenges that they were facing as a result of the discovery and how they were not benefitting anything from this resource. All these stories were captured in the exhibition which actively sought to address inequalities that had arisen in Chiadzwa. Resultantly, there was a paradigm shift which saw our museum discarding the old colonial outlook and adopting a new museological practice that increased relevance through public engagement, participation and more inclusive forms of representation.

The use of the museum as an engagement zone for active adult learning was borrowed from the concept of contact zone which was developed by Pratt (1992) as a space of exchange, action and transaction carried out within the spirit of reciprocity. In the same manner, the museum's deploying of local voices in a museum exhibition made the museum a typical space of collective meaning making, co-knowledge production and a praxis for social- and self-reflexivity (Clover et al. 2016). More importantly, by integrating the local experiences with educational aspects around mining, the museums become pedagogical institutions that give communities spaces to explore controversial issues collectively (Banz 2008). In this sense, we transformed the museum exhibitions from being more than just sites for the manifestation of preconceived curatorial theory into what museum space into what Butler and Lehrer (2016) described as sites of collaborative research and knowledge production, where the exhibitions shift from the status of merely presenting concluded results into important active venues for analysing social issues and for producing new relevant knowledge (Dahre 2019; Hansen, Henningsen and Gregersen 2019). This is in contrast with the colonial approach where museum curators with their connoisseurial knowledge used to operate as discrete and invisible exhibition makers sometimes completely detached from the societies and cultures which they were studying or interpreting (Arero and Kingdon 2005: Hansen, Henningsen and Gregersen 2019). Thus, the collaborative approach gives room for more participatory and co-creative exhibition making practices, allowing communities an opportunity for self-representation, and at the same time making the museums more relevant to the communities in which they are located.

Conclusion

In our thinking, through the diamond mining exhibition co-curated in collaboration with the local communities, we used new museological approaches as pedagogical and decolonial practices that allowed the Chiadzwa community to be actively involved in the production of narratives about their experiences of a controversial social issue. Perhaps as articulated by Hutchison (2013: 145) this "new museology is one way of describing a body of practical and theoretical museum work that takes account of the way museums position cultures and social identities in their collections and exhibitions and of the way they interact with their publics." As proposed on the notions of new museology, we had rendered an inclusive process that enhanced democratic learning and inclusive practices that involves developing collaborative relationships societies and communities (Vergo 1989; Clive 2005). Inspired by the idea of a "new museology" (Vergo 1989; Clive 2005), partly understood as a pedagogical discourse around the social and political roles of museums that encourages new communication and new styles of expression in contrast to classic, collections-centred museum models, we opened up our curatorial practices to a marginalized section of society. While the power relations could still be described as asymmetrical and in favour of the museum as an institution, the active participation of local communities in the curation of the exhibition and in creating interest in the exhibition showed how the relationship between communities, their learning needs and knowledge was amplified to enable a new process in which the museum and communities become equal partners as well as controlling agents in the project (Message 2013). We deem these new museology approaches to be central tenets of critical decolonial strategies which question and deconstruct the Eurocentric idea of museums as storehouses and destabilize power relations between museums and the communities that they serve (Stam 1993). These approaches reflect greater awareness of the social and political role of museums and encompass meaningful community collaboration in curatorial practices (McCall and Gray 2014). They question traditional museum approaches to issues of value, meaning, control, interpretation, authority and authenticity. Whereas in the old museology Mutare Museum was imagined as a repository of dominant cultures, in this dimension of a new museology, the museum advocated for its opening as a democratic space which offers diverse learning choices to the community.

Notes

1 Chiadzwa diamond fields are located approximately 80 miles southwest of the city of Mutare, Manicaland, Zimbabwe.

2 The Marange diamond fields are an area of widespread small-scale diamond production in Chiadzwa, Mutare District, Zimbabwe. Although estimates of the reserves contained in this area vary wildly, some have suggested that it could be home to one of the world's richest diamond deposits. The hugely prolific fields are regarded by some experts as the world's biggest diamond (in carats, not by value) find in more than a century. Production from Marange is controversial due to ongoing legal wrangles and government crackdowns on illegal miners and allegations of forced labour. In terms of carats produced, the Marange field is the largest diamond producing project in the world, estimated to have produced 16.9 million carats in 2013, or 13% of global rough diamond supply. Marange is estimated to have produced 12.0 million carats in 2012, 8.7 million carats in 2011, and 8.2 million carats in 2010.

3 *The Manica Post* is a state-run newspaper that is wholly owned by the government and is a subsidiary of Zimbabwe Papers; the publisher of other pro-state newspapers, namely The Herald, *The Chronicle* and *The Sunday Mail. The Manica Post* mainly covers news coming out

of Eastern Zimbabwe and is a weekly (Friday) publication. Zimbabwe Television (ZTV) is a subsidiary of Zimbabwe Broadcasting Cooperation (ZBC), a state-controlled electronic media company that runs the only television station in the country together with four radio stations – Radio Zimbabwe, National FM, Spot FM and Power FM.

4 Spanning about 60 000 hectares, Marange diamond fields are widely considered to be the biggest find of alluvial diamonds in the history of mankind. From the early 1980s, De Beers held an Exclusive Prospecting Order (EPO) over Marange via its subsidiary company, Kimberlitic Searches Limited (Ministry of Mines 2003). De Beers geologists started prospecting for kimberlite in the area in 2001 and discovered alluvial diamonds in 2002. De Beers' exploration certificate expired in March 2006 and was not renewed (Ministry of Mines 2003). In June 2006 some villagers, having worked under De Beers, started mining in the area, which led to a diamond rush and the invasion of the fields by people from all over the country.

Bibliography

Arero, H. and Kingdon, Z. 2005. Introduction: Visual Culture and Creativity in Eastern Africa: Reviewing a Neglected Branch of the Discipline. In H. Arero and Kingdon, Z (eds). *East African Contours: Reviewing Creativity and Visual Arts*. London: The Horniman Museum and Gardens, pp. 1–5.

Banz, R. (2015). Self-Directed Learning: Implications for Museums. *Journal of Museum Education* 33(1): 43–54.

Bell, L., and Clover, D. E. (2017). Critical Culture: Environmental Adult Education in Public Museums. *New Directions For Adult and Continuing Education* 153: 17–29.

Brady, L. and Crouch J. (2010). Partnership archaeology and indigenous ancestral engagement in Torres Strait, North-eastern Australia." In J. Laydon and U. Z. Rizvi (eds). *Handbook of Postcolonial Archaeology*. Walnut Creek, CA: Walnut Creek, pp. 413–428.

Burdick, J. and Sandlin, J. A. (2013). Learning, becoming, and the unknowable: Conceptualisations, mechanisms and process in public pedagogy literature. *Curriculum Inquiry* 43 (1): 142–177.

Butler, S. and Lehrer, E. (2016). Introduction: Curatorial Dreaming. In S. R. Butler and E. Lehrer (eds). *Curatorial Dreams*. London: McGill-Queen's University Press, pp. 3–26.

Clover, D. A. (2015). Adult Education for Social and Environmental Change in Contemporary Public Art Galleries and Museums in Canada, Scotland and England. *International Journal of Lifelong Education* 34 (3–3): 300–315

Clover, D. E., Sanford, K., Johnson, K., and Bell, L. (2016). Introduction. In D. E Clover, K. Stanford, L. Bell and K. Johnson (eds.), *Adult Education, Museums and Art Galleries: Animating Social, Cultural and Institutional Change*. Rotterdam, The Netherlands: Sense Publishers, pp. vii–xxi.

Chipangura, N. (2019). *Ngoda*: The Wealth Beneath Our Feet Exhibition: An Adult Education Practice at Mutare Museum, Eastern Zimbabwe. *The Canadian Journal for the Study of Adult Education* 31 (2): 51–58.

Chipangura, N., Bond, P., and Sack, S. 2020. Critical representations of Southern African Inequality: Transcending outmoded exhibition and museum politics. *Development Southern Africa* 36 (6): 767–787.

Chipangura, N. and Marufu, H. (2019). Museums as public forums for 21st century societies: A perspective of the National Museums and Monuments of Zimbabwe. In R. Janes and R. Sandell (eds). *Museum Activism*. London: Routledge, pp. 164–173.

Gable, E. (2013). The City, Race and the Creation of a Common History at the Virginia Historical Society. In V. Golding and W. Modest (eds). *Museums and Communities: Curators, Collections, and Collaboration*. London: Bloomsbury Academic, pp. 32–48.

Golding, V. (2016). *Learning at the Museum Frontiers: Identity Race and Power*. London: Routledge.

Gukurume, S. and Nhodo, L. (2020). Forced Displacements in Mining Communities: Politics in Chiadzwa Diamond Area, Zimbabwe. *Journal of Contemporary African Studies* 38 (1–1): 39–54.

Grenier, R. S. and Hafsteinsson, S. B. (2016). Shut Up and Be Quiet! Icelandic Museums' Promotion of Critical Public Pedagogy and the 2008 Financial Crisis. In D. E. Clover, K. Stanford, L. Bell, and K. Johnson (eds.). *Adult Education, Museums and Art Galleries: Animating Social, Cultural and Institutional Change*. Rotterdam: Sense Publishers, pp. 3–14.

Hansen, M. Henningsen, A, and Gregersen, A. (2019). Introduction. In M. V. Hansen, A. F. Henningsen and A. Gregersen (eds). *Curatorial Challenges: Interdisciplinary Perspectives on Contemporary Curating*. London: Routledge, pp. 1–6.

Harrison, F. V. (2009). Reworking African(ist) Archaeology in the Postcolonial Period: A Sociocultural Anthropologist's Perspective. In P. R. Schmidt (ed). *Postcolonial Archaeologies in Africa*. Santa Fe, NM: School for Advanced Research Press, pp. 231–242.

Hutchison, M. (2013). Shared Authority: Collaboration, Curatorial Voice and Exhibition Design in Canberra, Australia. In V. Golding and W. Modest (eds). *Museums and Communities: Curators, Collections and Collaborations*. London: Bloomsbury, pp. 143–162.

Janes, R. and Sandell, R. (2019). Posterity has arrived: The necessary emergence of museum activism in R. Janes and R. Sandell (eds). *Museum Activism*, London: Routledge, pp. 1–22.

Karp, I. (1991). Festivals. In I. Karp and S. D. Lavine (eds). *Exhibiting Cultures: The Poetics and Politics of Museum Display*. Washington, DC: Smithsonian Institute, pp. 119–127.

Karp, I. and Kratz, C.A. (2014). The Interrogative Museum. In R. Silverman (ed). *Translating Knowledge: Global Perspectives on Museum Community*. New York: Routledge, pp. 279–299.

McCall, V. and Gray, C. (2014). Museums and the 'new Museology': Theory, Practice and Organisational Change. *Museum Management and Curatorship* 29 (1–1): 19–35.

Meskell, L. (2009). Introduction. In L. Meskell (ed). *Cosmopolitan Archaeologies*. Durham, NC: Duke University Press, pp. 1–28.

Message, K. (2013). *Museums and Social Activism: Engaged Protests*. London: Routledge.

Ministry of Mines. (2013). The Geology of Marange. Ministry of Mines and Minerals Development, Zimbabwe.

Ndlovu, N. (2009). Decolonising the Mind-Set: South African Archaeology in a Postcolonial, Post-Apartheid Era. In P. R. Schmidt (ed). *Postcolonial Archaeologies in Africa*. Santa Fe, NM: School for Advanced Research Press, pp. 177–192.

Nyamunda, T. and Mukwambo, P. (2012). The State and the Bloody Diamond Rush in Chiadzwa: Unpacking the Contesting Interests in the Development of Illicit Mining and Trading, C. 2006—2009. *Journal of Southern African Studies* 38 (1–1): 145–166.

Onciul, B. (2015). *Museums, Heritage and Indigenous Voice: Decolonising Engagement*. London: Routledge.

Peers, L. and Brown, A. K. (2003). Introduction. In L. Peers and A. K. Brown (eds). *Museums and Source Communities*. London: Routledge, pp. 1–17.

Sandell, R. (2002). Museums and the Combating of Social Inequality: Roles, Responsibilities, Resistance. In Sandell, R. (ed). *Museums, Society, Inequality*. London: Routledge, pp. 3–24.

Sandell, R. (2007). *Museums, Prejudice, and the Reframing of Difference*. London: Routledge.

Sandell, R. (2017). *Museums, Moralities and Human Rights*. London: Routledge.

Schmidt, P. R. (2009). What Is Postcolonial About Archaeologies in Africa? In P. R. Schmidt (ed). *Postcolonial Archaeologies in Africa*. Santa Fe, NM: School for Advanced Research Press, pp. 1–20.

Segobye, A. K. (2009). Between Indigene and Citizen: Locating the Politics of the Past in Postcolonial Southern Africa. In P. R. Schmidt (ed). *Postcolonial Archaeologies in Africa*. Santa Fe, NM: School for Advanced Research Press, pp. 163–176.

Silverman, L. H. (2010). *The Social Work of Museums*. London: Routledge.

Simon, N. (2009). The Participatory Museum. Retrieved January 2, 2019 from http://www.participatorymuseum.org/read/

Stam, C. (1993). The Informed Muse: The Implications of 'the New Museology' for Museum Styles, C. (2011). Dialogic Learning in Museum Space. *Ethos* 19 (3): 12–20.

Vawda, S. (2019). Museums and the Epistemology of Injustice: From Colonialism to Decoloniality. *Museum International* 71 (281–282): 72–79.

Vergo, P. (1989). Introduction. In Vergo, P. (ed). *The New Museology*. London: Reaktion, pp. 1–6.

Watson, S. (2007). Museums and Their Communities. In S. Watson (ed). *Museums and Their Communities*. London: Routledge, pp. 1–25.

3 Heritage, communities and collaborative involvement at Matendera archaeological site

Introduction

Matendera festival is a ceremony conducted annually to celebrate the intangible heritage of the Shona people of Buhera in eastern Zimbabwe, popularly known as the *Vahera*, through their native dances, traditional music and cuisine, and a marathon. The ceremony is hosted annually at Matendera, a spectacular dry-stone-walled Iron Age site whose builders are historically connected to the *Vahera* (Chipangura et al. 2019). Through coordinating the efforts of Mutare Museum, the Buhera Rural District Council (BRDC) and other secondary stakeholders, the *Vahera* community gathers at Matendera to showcase their traditional foods, dances and games as part of their efforts to celebrate and experience Hera history and culture in relation to the tangible aspects of Matendera, a former abode of their ancestors. We argue that the new forms of engagement with local communities at this site encapsulate decolonial practices, particularly in the way they coalesce around inclusivity, where the local community has a higher degree of participation and agency in the interpretation of their cultural heritage (Chipangura and Chipangura 2020: 11). Through such activities the expert-community dichotomy as promoted by colonially inherited heritage practices was unsettled, resulting in the expansion of audiences and the promotion and foregrounding of previously marginalized cultural practices and ways of knowing.

Community archaeology and community collaboration

Collaborations are at the centre of decolonial initiatives since they promote engagement over doctrine and multivocality over connoisseurship (Boast 2011). Collaborations ensure that communities are not considered as passive audiences for didactic and authoritative forms of knowledge production but are implicated in an ongoing process of knowledge production and debate as active co-producers (Butler and Lehrer 2016: De Palma 2019; Henningsen and Gregersen 2019). Community archaeology as a form of collaborative project is a movement away from the traditional colonial model of archaeology in that it is a socially and politically self-conscious mode of research that incorporates different cultural perspectives in the interpretation of the past (see Smith 2007; Colwell-Chanthaphonh and Ferguson 2008; Brady and Crouch 2010). Although community archaeology can have many definitions and forms, it can be regarded as a social commitment to contemporary society. It is also a dialogue regarding the participation of indigenous communities and the diversification of spaces in which archaeological discourses are circulated (Matsuda and Okamura 2011). Furthermore, and as argued by Vilches et al. (2015: 375), this is a new method of archaeology that is situated in the present and is informed by a critical reflection which recognizes that archaeology as a practice is intertwined in a fabric of social and political relations. At the Matendera archaeological site, Mutare Museum managed to build a mutually beneficial relationship with local communities through collaborating with them in an annual festival – a living practice developed and promoted around an archaeological site.

The collaborative approach decentred archaeology's disciplinary authority by allowing for an investigative process in which decision making about heritage conservation became a shared responsibility with local communities. As a result, diverse perspectives emerged in the interpretation of the Matendera site with more than one significance, origin and/or use (Vilches et al. 2015). We argue that collaborations are an important strategy of decolonizing archaeological practice. A decolonizing agenda informed by community engagement means that archaeologists are no longer the sole authoritative voice but rather are partners in joint ventures in which stories about the past shift from one particular expert reading to the way they are told, circulated and received by the community (Haber and Gnecco 2007; Bruchac 2014). Thus, collaborative approaches lead to what Anton Haber (2012) terms an "un-disciplining" of archaeological practice which confront and challenge long-standing imbalances regarding who makes decisions and who benefits. Bruchac (2014: 2069) argues that "decolonising approaches in archaeology emerged as a means to counter the dominance of colonial ideologies and to improve the accuracy of indigenous representations." Hence at Matendera, decolonized archaeologies offered positive alternatives to colonial era theories by exploring African quests for identities that speak on local knowledge and also render the archaeological practice relevant to individual and collective well-being (Bugarin 2009; Harrison 2009; Schmidt 2009; Segobye 2009).

However, it is also important to stress that community engagements do not completely reject tenets of scientific inquiry, but rather challenge the legacy of colonialism and the hegemony of Western knowledge (Nicholas and Watkins 2014). Supernant and Warrick (2014: 563) also support the notion that using indigenous, collaborative and community-oriented approaches in archaeological research and practice is a path towards the decolonization of archaeology. To decolonize archaeology means that decisions, objectives and outcomes of archaeological research are in the hands of or are developed in partnership with local communities (Supernant and Warrick 2014). Some of the key decolonizing strategies, as Bruchac (2014: 2069) proposes, include "critical analysis of social and political relations, collaborative consultation and research design, reclamation of cultural landscapes and heritage sites, repatriation of human remains, co-curation of archaeological collections, and devising more culturally accurate museum representations." "Community archaeology" and "indigenous archaeology" often appear as interchangeable terms. This is another decolonizing initiative that incorporates native people not as subjects but as equal collaborators, and aims to challenge the master narrative by decentring the archaeological practice and giving indigenous people the power to set the research agenda, ask questions and circulate social knowledge that reflects their own traditional methods (Supernant and Warrick, 2014). Thus, according to Colwell-Chanthaphonh and Ferguson:

> ... collaborative research responds to the shortcomings of scientific investigations that disregard communities that are affected by the research process – it is an attempt to restore fairness to archaeological practice by aspiring to create benefits for both practitioners of sciences and its subjects. (Colwell-Chanthaphonh and Ferguson 2008: 7)

Some have argued that collaborative or community archaeology is a specific type of indigenous archaeology that hinges on multivocal archaeological research with indigenous communities (Supernant and Warrick 2014). Decolonization, as Bruchac (2014: 2070) posits, is an essential component of indigenous archaeology and at its basic level of analysis it questions the application of binary choices used in categorising and classifying archaeological finds. However, the notion of a community itself is not timeless nor is it a homogenous whole because it often embodies a lot of contradictions and incoherence as identities tend to shift, overlap, slide and change (Pyburn 2003; Smith 2007). The heterogeneous nature of a community means that there can be problems and challenges associated within the application of collaborative archaeology. In this regard, Colwell-Chanthaphonh and Ferguson (2008) succinctly argue that collaboration itself is not one uniform idea or a practice but rather is a range of strategies that moves archaeology as a discipline towards more accurate, inclusive and ethically sound practices. Collaborative methods in archaeology have been critiqued by La Salle (2010), who argues that they still produce unequal exercises of power and self-referential knowledge because in most cases the researched community has no control over the information extracted. Hence, despite the good intentions of making collaborations a decolonial strategy, this actually perpetuates the same exploitations inherent in traditional archaeological research (La Salle 2010). She critiques collaboration as a fancy new buzzword full of inequity with no consensus of what it actually entails (La Salle 2010: 413). Therefore, we also admit that archaeology as a discipline is inherently powerful and even when we work with local communities there is still potential for uneven distribution of power and disenfranchising of the same communities.

Engaging communities: the Matendera cultural festival

The Matendera archaeological site is situated within Buhera District, a semi-arid landscape which forms the middle veld of the Zimbabwe Plateau (see Figure 3.1). This rural district is largely populated by indigenous Shona communities whose livelihood is based on subsistence agriculture and livestock rearing (Lindahl and Matenga 1995). In present-day Zimbabwe, the term Shona is generally used to refer to the indigenous Bantu communities that speak a similar language (Beach 1980; Chimhundu 1992; Chirikure et al. 2017). In Buhera, the contemporary Shona communities largely speak the Karanga and Manyika dialects, and their ancestry is largely associated with a cluster of ancient dry-stone-walled palaces, popularly known to the Shona community as *madzimbabhwe* or *madzimbabwe* (houses of stone), and to Africanists as the "Zimbabwe culture" (CE 1000–1900) (Caton-Thompson 1931; Garlake 1970; Beach 1980; Lindahl and Matenga 1995; Huffman 1996, 2007; Pikirayi 2001; Chirikure et al. 2012). Matendera is the largest known *dzimbahwe* (singular) within the Buhera cluster (Caton-Thompson 1931; Lindahl and Matenga 1995). Its architecture is believed to be the most impressive within

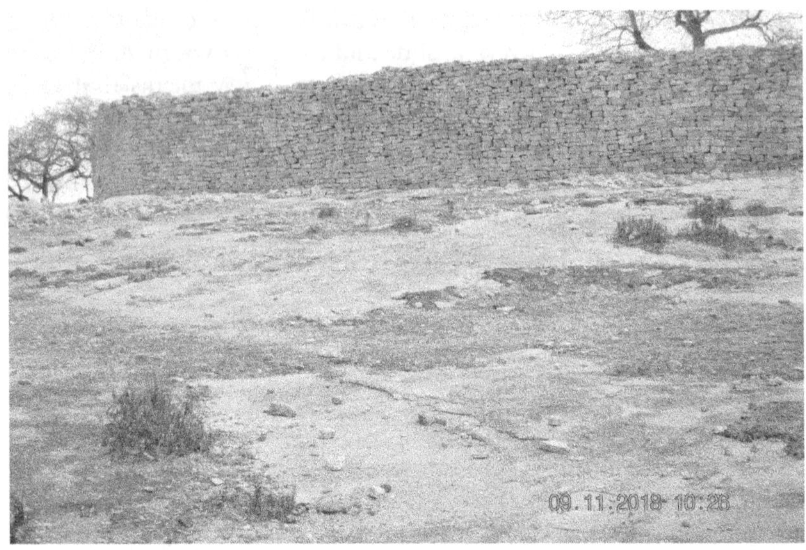

Figure 3.1 Matendera archaeological site. Photograph by Njabulo Chipangura.

the region (Huffman 1996): it consists of rough dry-stone-walled free-standing enclosures with dentelle and herringbone decoration (Caton-Thompson 1931). According to Huffman (1996: 160–164), as at Great Zimbabwe, the largest known *dzimbabwe* in sub-Saharan Africa, the spatial organisation at Matendera was arranged in a lay-out that accommodated both elites and commoners. Nevertheless, because of royal privilege, elite residences were constructed within the walled areas, whilst the commoners lived outside the walls. Huffman's description aptly gives a bird's eye view of the architectural make-up of the site and its probable use, although the elite/commoner division has been deeply contested as a hegemonic archaeological discourse in the last two decades (Chirikure et al. 2018). An annual festival is held by the community, working together with Mutare Museum, the BRDC and other stakeholders, to celebrate Matendera as community heritage. The festival is an inclusive discourse underpinned by multiple voices, multiple intersections and a nexus of cultural and stakeholder communities. The first author, Njabulo Chipangura has been instrumental in working with communities in organizing this festival since its inception in 2010.

In light of this background, we engaged various communities who attended the annual festivals (2010–2018) in conversations about the intangible meanings and importance of the Matendera festival, using an "archaeological ethnographical model" that consisted of standard interactive discussions, conversations and participant observations. Archaeological ethnography is described by Hollowell and Mortensen (2009: 7) as "the implications of archaeologised places, pasts, and ideas for others, and how people make these things their own." In essence, we argue that the festival is about relational and procedural intangible social activities that work towards a state of equilibrium by bringing people into direct contact with their heritage. At the same time, it is also about understanding and practicing shared authority in heritage conservation and presentation. Archaeological ethnography has also been defined by Hamilakis, Anagnostopoulos and Ifantidis (2009: 284) as "... a transdisciplinary, transcultural space for critical engagement and dialogue which enables an understanding of local unofficial contemporary discourses and practices to do with archaeological sites." Thus, using data drawn from interviews and participant observations, we argue that Matendera as an archaeological site cannot be divorced from the intangible socio-cultural practices that are being followed there in the form of traditional dances, music, poetry and the preparation and consumption of traditional cuisines during the

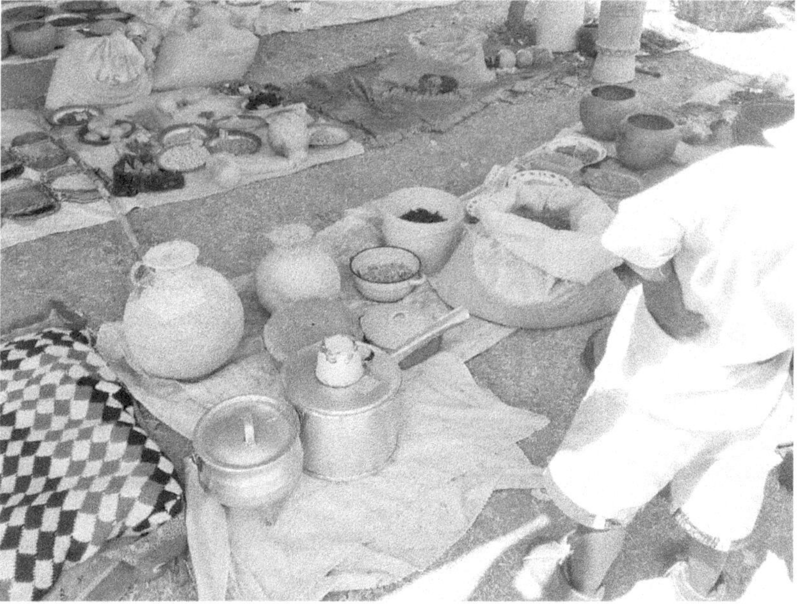

Figure 3.2 Activities during Matendera festival – a display of various local cultural wares. Photograph by Njabulo Chipangura.

festival. Consequently, we reveal the reality that the Matendera community does not privilege the grand or the material in their day-to-day use of the site as may be implied by archaeologists but rather brings a range of intangible associations with diachronic values (Smith 2006).

According to the information gathered from interviewees from the heritage community during our research, the name Matendera is derived from the Shona word *tenderera* which denotes the circular shape of the monument. However, apart from the name that the community easily identify themselves with, the hegemonic discourse about the site encompasses all the grand narratives presented and derived from expert knowledge (i.e. Caton-Thompson 1931; Huffman 1996; Pikirayi 2001) as is exhibited in guided tours and the ethics of technical conservation. As such, this discourse is embedded in aspects of monumentality and aesthetics at the expense of intangible socio-cultural processes, as well as the ideas that led to the construction of the site (Smith 2014). Basically, the discourse is underwritten by archaeological evidence which has been interpreted to show that the site was constructed between the sixteenth and eighteenth centuries. According to previous archaeological research, the archaeological site of Matendera was built on a low-domed kopje of smooth granite as a royal palace (Caton-Thompson 1931; Huffman 1996), and that Matendera constitutes part of what is called the "Buhera cluster" of Zimbabwe sites (Hall 1987; Huffman 1996; Pikirayi 2001).

The other archaeological sites in this cluster are the Chiona, Kagumbudzi and Muchuchu sites, which have been declared national monuments. It is argued that the same people who built Great Zimbabwe were involved in the construction of Matendera (Huffman 1996). Similarity in the construction techniques and the dressing of the walls with decorations such as herringbone and dentelle provide the basis for this argument. Extrapolation of this hegemonic discourse is also seen in a "one size fits all" approach in which restorations are carried out at the site guided by specific scientific principles that are deployed in the service of authenticity and a respect for the historicity of all Zimbabwe cultural monuments in southern Africa (see Chirikure, 2014).

However, in spite of the prevalence of scientific research and interpretations of Matendera as a site, the idea of carrying out a festival can be understood as an attempt by the heritage community to respond to these popular archaeological interpretations by offering their own alternative story of the past through song, dance, poetry and traditional cuisine. It is an attempt to use performance to imagine the site's values that go beyond the scientific and the material as espoused by experts. The fact that the festival started off as a community project can be regarded as a bottom-up response to the authorised official narratives. This festival confers an alternative dimension to conventional archaeology and heritage management by empowering the local community. However, for Mutare Museum, the festival presented a good opportunity for integrating and promoting community-based values of the archaeological site, perhaps engendering a form of community archaeology which, as argued by Atalay (2012: 5), provides a method for a community and archaeologists to work together to pursue a research design that benefits them as equal partners. Using this method, there is continuous engagement in which archaeologists and community members collaboratively define the questions, methods and outcomes of a given project (Colwell 2016: 116), where the sharing power with indigenous communities gets used to pluralise, democratise and decolonise relations (Schmidt 2009; Onciul 2015). Community archaeology has become a popular decolonializing strategy that is being used at many heritage sites in Africa. On the whole, decolonised methodologies can be applied to heritage practice by embracing the so-called "unofficial narratives" of non-experts and promoting an understanding of how to listen and pay attention to subaltern voices (Bugarin 2009; Harrison 2009; Meskell 2007; Ndlovu 2009; Segobye 2009; Schmidt 2009; Taruvinga and Ndoro 2003). Today, across the global networks of heritage sites, museums and galleries, the importance of communities to the interpretation and preservation of heritage is increasingly being recognised (Watson 2007; Tunbridge and Ashworth 1996).

For the Mutare Museum, participating in the Matendera festival over the last eight years engendered a decolonial practice which is different from and responded to the static nature of museum displays (Flint 2006). Whereas in museums the focus is on displaying material objects, the ambience and dynamism of festivals makes them more participatory, oriented towards action and performance (Bauman and Sawin 1991). The Matendera festival has become a celebration of the multiple forms of intangible heritage of the *Vahera* expressed through their traditional dances such as *mhande*, traditional music and the preparation of traditional dishes. The festival opens the space for the community to participate in the conservation and presentation of their intangible cultural heritage. The festival is largely curated by local communities working through a collaborative partnership with BRDC. The museum is an important stakeholder which facilitates the hosting of the festival at Matendera and allows for conversations around local protection of both tangible and intangible heritage. Over the past 10 years, the participation of children from nearby schools, traditional dancers, choir groups, traditional cuisine groups and athletes has enriched the festival.

In so many ways, a festival of this nature devolves power from authorised institutions to the local population, with emphasis placed on community ownership of heritage resources. In this festival, power and authority are concentrated in the hands of the community in which the agency of the participants themselves is recognised. The Matendera community was given an opportunity for self-representation through a working partnership with Mutare Museum. Collaborative activities of this sort are not only beneficial to the community, but to Mutare Museum, because they often mitigate heritage conflicts (Harrison and Hughes 2005). Instead of creating a dichotomy between communities and authorities, the Matendera festival can be regarded as a typical example of a shared authority platform. The festival offers alternative narratives of the past through song, dance, poetry and the preparation and consumption of traditional dishes. Representing their ways of life in an open festival setting also gives the community an opportunity to conserve and transmit their intangible cultural heritage to future generations.

During the festival, communities also take full control of representing their intangible cultural practices. Witz (2003) argues that the euphoria associated with a festival usually generates alternative modes of interpretation which are different from official authorised discourses. Dance, and the rhythms of the past through belting out traditional music, are imparted or transmitted to future generations only if they are constantly recited and performed – hence the festival provides a platform for such continuity. This festival has a social dimension in which parts of the community are brought into contact with each other in various activities. Lavenda (1992: 81) also argues that "because many festival events are undemanding, it is easy for a wide range of people to attend and enjoy them and come away with the feeling that they are part of an organic, harmonious community." As a result, the chances are increased for people to develop mutual empathy and understandings which reduce conflicts about heritage. The Matendera festival also contributes towards the conservation and sustainable management of cultural resources through the protection of local heritage and a revitalisation of indigenous culture, arts and crafts.

Collaboration, self-representation and social cohesion at Matendera

The inaugural Matendera festival was held in October 2010 as a community initiative, with localised celebrations taking place at the site, led by the village heads. Anchored in wholesome and inclusive community participation, it managed to improve the preservation and transmission of intangible cultural and historical traditions. Furthermore, it allowed for engagement and active community participation which is markedly different from the conservation tropes of the authorised heritage discourse. Compared to the hegemonic discourses driven by "expert" knowledge, festivals tell decolonial stories that ignore universalizing themes in that they often speak to the cultural experiences of marginalised groups (Karp and Kratz 1991). Therefore festivals, by their very nature, leave room for the community to ascribe multiple meanings to their heritage, taken from their own diverse points of understanding. Festivals also place an emphasis on the idea of oneness and collaboration, rather than distinction, as members of a particular community tend to share a world view during the celebrations (Witz 2003).

During this festival, *Vahera* people commemorate their cultural diversity in relation to the tangible aspects of Matendera monument. Thus, unlike in the authorised heritage discourse which is preoccupied by materiality, innate significance and expert judgement, this festival does not distinguish, separate or dichotomise the tangible and the intangible heritage, but rather looks at both of them as mutually constitutive (Smith 2006). For these communities, the material aspects of the site are only a part of the spiritual and religious values. Upheld by societies over many centuries, against the onslaught of modernisation, the spiritual values well regarded by the local community, and the associated ritual practice which takes place on the site during the festival and other moments during the year, are seen as the raison d'etre of the physical monument. Through these on-site practices of pastness, the intangible heritage as values and practices invokes a sense of inclusion and the recognition of a living heritage, and carries with it the meanings ascribed to material sites by non-professionals. According to UNESCO, intangible cultural heritage does not only represent inherited traditions from the past but also contemporary rural and urban practices in which diverse cultural groups take part. Thus, the Matendera festival can be regarded as a contemporary form of Intangible Cultural Heritage (ICH)typified by socio-cultural practices that are still being undertaken, in the form of traditional dances, music, poetry, the preparation of traditional foods and social games such as *nhodo*, *pada* and *tsoro* (Chipangura, Chiripanhura and Nyamagodo 2018). These performances enliven the site and engender a sense of ownership while allowing communities to promote their culture and traditions.

Apart from traditional dance and music, the Matendera festival is also celebrated with ball games, a marathon, and singing and cooking competitions. Usually three months prior to the festival, which is held in September each year, an organizing committee comprising village heads, school headmasters, the district administrator, non-governmental organisations (NGOs), Mutare Museum and BRDC convenes fortnightly. The coming together of different stakeholders in the organisation of this festival facilitates multisectoral and interdisciplinary dialogue about the safeguarding of tangible and intangible heritage (Galla 2016). In addition, standing subcommittees are formed in which different stakeholders are assigned tasks. Site clearing and guided tours on the day of the festival are assigned to Mutare Museum, whereas BRDC is mandated with transport services and road maintenance. Village and school heads coordinate various social events within their communities. These preparations are carried out at the nearest local primary and secondary schools. Village heads working with their respective communities also arrange for traditional foods to be prepared during the festival. Some of the commonly cooked foods include goat meat, okra, stiff sorghum and rapoko porridge, blackjack, dried cow bean leaves and pumpkin leaves with peanut butter, along with a host of other traditional dishes. A traditional brew is also prepared, mostly by village elders. The process of fermenting the sorghum, which is an essential ingredient of this brew, takes up to seven days. Imbibing the traditional beer is a popular activity during the festival, with drinking strictly reserved for persons over the age of 18. NGOs that operate in Buhera, such as CARE Zimbabwe, OXFAM and the Red Cross assist in providing prize money and other gifts that are given to the winning teams in the ball games and the marathon.

Each of the six villages that surround the Matendera site assembles a soccer team to compete in the knock-out stages of the Matendera Trophy. The Matendera 10 km open marathon is another activity which is popular amongst villagers during the festival. The most important thing to note is that although these two sporting activities are marked by some form of competition, people join in for fun, and everything is marked by a celebratory mood of one-ness. Therefore, the festival itself promotes social cohesion by bringing together people in one setting as they also share their life stories. Some might have lost contact over time, and the festival acts as a platform for reconnecting. According to Lavenda (1992), festivals provide a focal point for scheduling reunions and family get-togethers. Being in a rural setting, the Matendera festival also helps to reveal any sporting talents that villagers possess, and in some cases, budding stars are identified during both the soccer match and the marathon. Another big attraction during the festival is the women's singing and cooking competitions. Like the soccer tournament, each village assembles a team to participate in both sets of competitions. The cooking competition is based on a selected traditional dish, and the judges are drawn from elderly members of the community. For the singing competition, teams are given a traditional song one month before the festival to practice. The theme song is selected by village heads working together with the organising committee.

In 2014, this festival experienced unprecedented growth when the Matendera site hosted national celebrations for World Tourism Day on the theme "Tourism and Community Development." The national festival was attended by top government officials, including the Minister of Tourism and Hospitality, who was the guest of honour. An interactive discussion was also opened in which the Matendera community shared their historical connections with the site with the various stakeholders in attendance. However, although a festival is an ideal platform for promoting local intangible culture, there has been growing criticism that in some festivals the carnival atmosphere is exaggerated, and thus the occasion ends up losing its aura of being genuine and historic (Witz 2003; Karp and Kratz 1991). In such cases, the festival can inadvertently signal a staged authenticity made up of choreographed performances for consumption by the audience. Festivals of this nature tend to exaggerate and magnify events to achieve historical authenticity (Witz 2003; Karp and Kratz 1991; Flint 2006; Chipangura 2015). This somehow fits into what MacCannell (1973), describes as "staged authenticity" which entails a careful preparation of activities within cultural sites which do not reflect the historical narratives of such places. Furthermore, in some cases the intangible heritage, in the form of cultural performances, is vulnerable to manipulation through recreations which do not necessarily tally with the historical aspects of the site.

Decolonial knowledges: archaeological ethnographies and local knowledge

In using Archaeological ethnography to understand Matendera, we agree with Zager and Pluckhahn (2013: 48), who argue that "archaeologists have increasingly turned to ethnography as a tool for understanding the contemporary social context of material culture, archaeological practice, and decolonising archaeology." During the conversations and engagements with the community, it emerged that by carrying out this annual festival, the community gains a true sense of connection with their archaeological site. On the museum's part, a key collaborative aspect that was brought out during the festival was the installation of an exhibition in the "culture hut" at the site. In creating this exhibition, consultations were carried out with the community through group discussions on how they wanted the archaeological history of the site to be represented. During the designing of the exhibition, emphasis was also placed on co-curatorship which replaced the anonymous institutional voice with multiple voices telling the community's version of the past (Mallon 2019). The planning, presentation and interpretive methods used in this exhibition enabled the community to become actively involved in the representation of their own culture. In this way, community members and museum staff came together to develop the themes, temporal parameters and content of the exhibition. In this context, the community members were allowed to mount their own exhibitions, determining what would be on display and how it would be presented (Yerkovich 2016). As agreed with the local elders, the main aim of installing this exhibition was to uphold *Vahera* traditional cultural practices which were seen by the community as being in danger of extinction due to globalisation.

The inclusion of the community narratives challenged the museum's curatorial normative practices and thrust the museum into Hooper-Greenhill's (2007: 82) assertion that knowledge can no longer be considered to be unified and monolithic, but rather is fragmented and multi-vocal, in which a cacophony of voices may be heard. This assertion aptly resonates with the Matendera festival and the setting up of the exhibition. The exhibition was opened during the inaugural festival in 2010 with pictorial displays chronicling the archaeological history of the site. Archaeological objects that were excavated from the site (see Caton-Thompson 1931), including a collection of glass beads that had been kept at the Zimbabwe Museum of Human Sciences in Harare, which were exhibited, much to the delight of the community members in attendance. This was groundbreaking in that objects collected from a local site that had been centralized in a museum in a metropolitan city were "returned" to their place of origin. This return of the archaeological objects signified a shift, and a return of the local voices in the processes of knowledge production. Thus, knowledge production from this exhibition emerged as a shared responsibility between Mutare Museum and the community members whose narratives were included into the main storyline. Prior to this collaborative exhibition at Matendera, the main narrative had been based on conventional academic scholarship as presented through the lens of tour guides and curators. For many years, the transmission of knowledge at Matendera had been dominated by hegemonic archaeological narratives such as those from Caton-Thompson (1931) and Thomas Huffman (1996). The new developments made sure that during the festival and the making of the exhibition there was no prioritisation of the so-called "experts'" views, because emphasis was placed on non-hegemonic knowledge (Haber 2016; Lillios 2011). As a result, the festival, complemented by the exhibition, managed to tell the subaltern story of the heritage community.

During the festival and the exhibition, community members became the primary agents in determining the content presented. Archaeological ethnography thus came into focus as a concept and as a hybrid fieldwork method that investigated the multiple ways of creating knowledge at Matendera site. This, as we have illustrated, was achieved by working in collaboration with contemporary communities to decipher the micro-politics of archaeological practice (Meskell 2009; Witcomb 2007). In many ways, archaeological ethnography became a liberal platform of historical and cultural representation in which the community actively participated and showcased their varied cultural activities. One of the interviewees, a respected village head, said this during the inaugural festival:

> Matendera is our heritage, the site belongs to us because it was constructed by our ancestors. This festival is a welcome development in this village because it allows us to tell our stories about this site, using music, dance, poetry, and thereby we can be recognised as the rightful custodians of the site. Even in the past our forefathers used to carry out these activities at the site so I don't see the reason why we should be limited to use the site on festivals only. This is a living site with living values that survives outside the stone walls that you see here, and we must use it every day. (Headman Zvavahera, 16 August 2010, Matendera).

From this account by Headman Zvavahera, it can be argued that numerous perspectives and values can be brought together to enhance a shared understanding of the past (Davis 2007; Colwell 2016). In a way, archaeological ethnography de-centralises archaeological interests by focusing on building relationships from local narratives that do not always have to revolve around the official story. These narratives present contemporary local stories on an equal footing with established archaeological narratives (Stroulia and Sutton 2009).

Conclusion

This chapter has shown how strategies of archaeological ethnography, regarded as an assemblage of approaches which are informed by ethnographic engagements at heritage sites (Hamilakis and

Anagnostopoulos 2009; Zager and Pluckhahn 2013; Harrison 2016), can be deployed to make linkages between experts, archaeological sites and local communities, creating relationships that improve the interpretation and preservation of sites. During our research, archaeological ethnography was deployed at Matendera site as a holistic form of anthropology which was improvisational, context-dependent and a decolonised methodology that embraced the so-called unofficial narratives from non-experts (Meskell 2005; Meskell 2007; Castaneda 2008; Colwell 2016; Haber 2016; Hamilakis 2016; Zimmerman 2005). The museum's engagement with communities using a cultural festival performed in situ at an archaeological site that is managed by the museum acknowledged local community members as active knowledge agents possessing their own epistemic understandings and readings of hegemonic discourses. The conservation manifest in resilient traditional systems and local ways of knowing embedded within community cultural practices, rituals and other religious prescripts that continue to play a role in preservation.

This deconstructed the expert-community dichotomy, allowing for a symbiotic engagement and acknowledgement of both forms of knowledge as equally valuable. Headman Zvavahera's narrative clearly shows that community perceptions do not necessarily need to be authenticated by archaeological knowledge. Rather, these local ways of knowing are based on intangible oral narratives that have been passed down from generation to generation. The sites, outside of the museum, afford museums an opportunity to look beyond their normative functions and extend their audience and reach, challenging the hegemonic relationship embedded in the museums' past approaches.

Bibliography

Atalay, S. (2012). *Community – Based Archaeology: Research with, by and for Indigenous and Local Communities*. Berkeley, CA: University of California Press.

Bauman, R. and Sawin, D. (1991). The Politics of Participation in Folk Life Festivals. In I. Karp and S. D. Lavine (eds). *Exhibiting Cultures*. Washington, DC: Smithsonian Institution Press, pp. 288–313.

Beach, D. N. (1980). *The Shona and Zimbabwe 900–1850*. London: Heinemann.

Boast, R. (2011). Neocolonial Collaboration: Museum as Contact Zone Revisited. *Museum Anthropology* 34 (1–1): 56–70.

Boast, R. (2011). Neocolonial Collaboration: Museum as Contact Zone Revisited. *Museum Anthropology* 56 (1): 65–70.

Brady, L. and Crouch J. (2010). Partnership Archaeology and Indigenous Ancestral Engagement in Torres Strait, North-Eastern Australia. In J. Laydon and U. Z. Rizvi (eds). *Handbook of Postcolonial Archaeology*. Walnut Creek, CA: Walnut Creek, pp. 413–428.

Bruchac, M. (2014). Decolonization in Archaeological Theory. In C. Smith. *Encyclopaedia of Global Archaeology*. New York: Springer, pp. 2069–2077.

Bugarin, F. T. (2009). Embracing Many Voices as Keepers of the Past. In P. R. Schmidt (ed). *Postcolonial Archaeologies in Africa*. Santa Fe, NM: School for Advanced Research Press, pp. 193–210.

Butler, S. and Lehrer, E. (2016). Introduction: Curatorial Dreaming. In S. R. Butler and E. Lehrer (eds). *Curatorial Dreams*. London: McGill-Queen's University Press, pp. 3–26.

Castaneda, Q. E. (2008). Ethnography and the Social Construction of Archaeology. In Q. E. Castaneda and C. N. Matthews (eds). *Ethnographic Archaeological Practices*. Lanham, MD: AltaMira Press, pp. 1–23.

Caton-Thompson, G. (1931). *The Zimbabwe Culture: Ruins and Reactions*. Oxford: Clarendon Press.

Chipangura, N. (2015). Representation, Reproduction and Transmission of Public Culture in Zimbabwean Museums, Commemorations and Festivals. In M. Mawere, H. Chiwaura and T. P. Thondhlana (eds). *African Museums in the Making: Reflections on the Politics of Material and Public Culture in Zimbabwe.* Bamenda: Langaa Publishers, pp. 68–83.

Chipangura, N. (2018). Cultural Heritage Sites and Contemporary Uses; Finding a Balance between Monumentality and Intangibility in Eastern Zimbabwe. In C. Waelde, C. Cummings, M. Pavis and H. Enright (eds). *Research Handbook on Contemporary Intangible Cultural Heritage Law and Heritage*. Cheltenham: Edward Elgar Publishing, pp. 379–398.

Chipangura, N., Bond, P., and Sack, S. (2020). Critical Representations of Southern African Inequality: Transcending Outmoded Exhibition and Museum Politics. *Development Southern Africa* 36 (6): 767–785.

Chipangura, N. and Chipangura, P. (2020). Community museums and rethinking the colonial frame of national museums in Zimbabwe. *Museum Management and Curatorship* 35 (1): 36–56.

Chipangura, N., Chiripanhura, P. and Nyamagodo, S. (2018). Policy Formulation and Collaborative Management: The Case of Ziwa Site, Eastern Zimbabwe. *Museum International* 69 (275–267–275–267): 116–123.

Chipangura, N., Nyamushosho, R., and Pasipanodya, T. (2019). Living site, living values: the Matendera festival as practice in community conservation and presentation. *International Journal of Intangible Heritage* 14 (1): 6–20.

Chirikure, S. (2014). Zimbabwe Culture before Mapungubwe: New Evidence from Mapela Hill, South – Western Zimbabwe. *PLOS* 10: pp. 1–18.

Chirikure, S., Manyanga, M. and Pollard, A. M. (2012). When Science Alone is Not Enough: Radiocarbon Timescales, History, Ethnography and Elite Settlements in Southern Africa. *Journal of Social Archaeology* 12 (3–3): 356–379.

Chirikure, S., Manyanga, M., Pollard, A. M., Bandama, F., Mahachi, G., Pikiraye, I. (2014). Zimbabwe Culture before Mapungubwe: New Evidence from Mapela Hill, South-Western Zimbabwe. *PLOS ONE* **9** (10): 1–18.

Chirikure, S., Nyamushosho, R., Bandama, F. and Dandara, C. 2018. Elites and Commoners at Great Zimbabwe: Archaeological and Ethnographic Insights on Social Power. *Antiquity* 92: 1056–1075.

Chirikure, S., Nyamushosho, R. T., Chimhundu, H. H., Dandara, C., Pamburai, H. H. and Manyanga, M. (2017). Concept and Knowledge Revision in the Post-Colony: Mukwerera, the Practice of Asking for Rain Amongst the Shona of Southern Africa. In M. Manyanga and S. Chirikure (eds). Bamenda: Langaa Publishers, pp. 34–49.

Colwell, C. (2016). Collaborative Archaeologies and Descendant Communities. *Annual Review of Anthropology* 45: 113–127.

Colwell-Chanthaphonh, C. and Ferguson, T. J. (eds). (2008). Introduction: The Collaborative Continuum. *Collaboration in Archaeological Practice, Engaging Descendant Communities*. Lanham: Altamira Press, pp. 1–35.

Davis, P. (2007). Place Exploration: Museums, Identity, Community. Communities. In S. Watson (ed). *Museums and Their Communities.* London: Routledge, pp. 53–76.

De Palma, M. (2019). Selfies, Yoga and Hip Hop: Expanding the Roles of Museums. In V. Golding and J. Walklate (eds). *Museums and Communities: Diversity, Dialogue and Collaborations in an Age of Migrations*. Cambridge: Cambridge Scholars Publishing, pp. 230–245.

Flint, L. (2006). Contradictions and Challenges in Representing the Past: The Kuomboka Festival of Western Zambia. *Journal of Southern African Studies* 32 (4–4): 701–717.

Galla, A. (2016). In the Search of the Inclusive Museum. In B. L. Murphy (ed). *Museums, Ethics and Cultural Heritage*. London and New York: Routledge, pp. 304–316.

Garlake, P. S. (1970). Rhodesian Ruins—A Preliminary Assessment of Their Styles and Chronology. *Journal of African History* 11 (4–4): 495–513.

Haber, A. (2012). Un-Disciplining Archaeology. *Archaeologies: Journal of the World Archaeological Congress* 8: 55–66.

Haber, A. (2016). Decolonising Archaeological Thought in South America. *Annual Review of Anthropology* 45: 469–485.

Haber, A. and Gnecco, C. 2007. Virtual Forum: Archaeology and Decolonization. *Archaeologies: Journal of the World Archaeological Congress* 3 (3): 390–412.

Hall, M. (1987). *The Changing Past: Farmers, Kings and Traders in Southern Africa 200-1860*. Cape Town: David Phillip.

Hamilakis, Y. (2016). Decolonial Archaeologies: From Ethnoarchaeology to Archaeological Ethnography. *World Archaeology* 48 (5): 678–682.

Hamilakis, Y. and Anagnostopoulos, A. (2009). What Is Archaeological Ethnography? *Public Archaeology: Archaeological Ethnographies* 8 (2–3–2–3): 65–87.

Hamilakis, Y., Anagnostopoulos, A. and Ifantidis, F. (2009). Postcards from the Edge of Time: Archaeology, Photography, Archaeological Ethnography (A Photo-Essay). *Public Archaeology: Archaeological Ethnographies* 8 (2–3–2–3): 283–309.

Hansen, M., Henningsen, A., and Gregersen, A. (2019). Introduction. In M. V. Hansen, A.F. Henningsen, and A. Gregersen (eds). *Curatorial Challenges: Interdisciplinary Perspectives on Contemporary Curating*. London: Routledge, pp. 1–6.

Harrison, F. V. (2009). Reworking African(1st) Archaeology in the Postcolonial Period: A Sociocultural Anthropologist's Perspective. In P. R. Schmidt (ed). *Postcolonial Archaeologies in Africa*. Santa Fe, NM: School for Advanced Research Press, pp. 231–242.

Harrison, R. (2016). Archaeologies of Emergent Presents and Futures. *Historical Archaeology* 50 (3–3): 165–180.

Harrison, R. and Hughes, L. (2010). *Understanding the Politics of Heritage: Global Heritage Perspective*. Manchester: Manchester University Press.

Hollowell, J. and Mortensen, L. (2009). Introduction: Ethnographies and Archaeologies. In L. Mortensen and J. Hollowell (eds). *Ethnographies and Archaeologies: Iterations of the Past.* Gainesville: Gainesville University Press of Florida, pp. 1–17.

Hooper-Greenhill, E. (2007). Interpretive Communities, Strategies and Repertoires. In S. Watson (ed). *Museums and Their Communities.* London: Routledge, pp. 76–95.

Huffman, T. N. (1996). *Snakes and Crocodiles: Power and Symbolism in Ancient Zimbabwe*. Johannesburg: Witwatersrand University Press.

Huffman, T. N. (2007). *Handbook to the Iron Age: The Archaeology of Pre-Colonial Farming Societies in Southern Africa*. Scottsville: University of KwaZulu-Natal Press.

Interview with Headman Zvavahera, 16 August 2010, Matendera Monument.

Karp, I. and Kratz, C. (1991). Festivals. In: I. Karp and S.D Lavine, eds, Exhibiting *Cultures; The Poetics and Politics of Museum Display*. Washington: Smithsonian Institution Press, pp. 28–58.

La Salle, M. 2010. Community Collaboration and Other Good Intentions. *Archaeologies* 6 (3): 401–422.

Lavenda, R. H. (1992). Festivals and Public Culture. In I. Karp, C. M. Kreamer and S. D. Lavine (eds). *Museums and Communities: The Politics of Public Culture.* Washington, DC: Smithsonian Institution Press, pp. 76–104.

Lillios, K. (2011). Archaeological Ethnographies by Yannis Hamilakis and Aris Anagnostopoulos, Editors. *Ethnoarchaeology* 3 (1–1): 107–110.

Lindahl, A. and Matenga, M. (1995). Present and Past: Ceramics and Homesteads: An Ethno-Archaeological Study in the Buhera District, Zimbabwe. *Studies in African Archaeology* 11. Department of Archaeology Uppsala: Uppsala University.

MacCannell, D. (1973). Staged Authenticity: Arrangements of Social Space in Tourist Settings. *The American Journal of Sociology* 79 (3–3): 589–603.

Mallon, S. (2019). *He alo a he alo/kanohi kit e kanohi/* Face to Face: Curatorial Bodies, Encounters and Relations. In P. Schorch, C. McCarthy, and E. Durr (eds). *Curatopia, Museums and the Future of Curatorship.* Manchester: Manchester University Press, pp. 89–98.

Matsuda, A. and Okamura. K. (2011). Introduction: New Perspectives in Global Public Archaeology. In K. Okamura and A. Matsuda (eds). *News Perspectives in Global Public Archaeology*. New York: Springer, pp. 1–18.

Meskell, L. (2005). Archaeological Ethnography: Conversations Around Kruger National Park. *Archaeologies* 1 (1–1): 81–100.

Meskell, L. (2007). Falling Walls and Mending Fences: Archaeological Ethnography in the Limpopo. *Journal of Southern African Studies* 33 (2–2): 383–400.

Meskell, L. (2009). Introduction. In L. Meskell (ed). *Cosmopolitan Archaeologies.* Durham, NC: Duke University Press, pp. 1–28.

Ndlovu, N. (2009). Decolonising the Mind-Set: South African Archaeology in a Postcolonial, Post-Apartheid Era. In P. R. Schmidt (ed). *Postcolonial Archaeologies in Africa.* Santa Fe, NM: School for Advanced Research Press, pp. 177–192.

Nicholas, G. and Watkins J. (2014). Indigenous Archaeologies in Archaeological Theory. In *C. Smith. Encyclopaedia of Global Archaeology*. New York: Springer. pp. 3777–3786.

Onciul, B. (2015). *Museums, Heritage and Indigenous Voice: Decolonising Engagement*. London: Routledge.

Pikirayi, I. (2001). *The Zimbabwe Culture: Origins and Decline of Southern Zambezian States*. Walnut Creek, CA: AltaMira Press.

Pyburn, K. A. (2003). Archaeology for a New Millennium: The Rules of Engagement. In L. Derry and M. Malloy (eds). *Archaeologists and Local Communities: Partners in Exploring the Past.* Washington, DC: Society for American Archaeology, pp. 167–184.

Schmidt, P. R. (2009). What Is Postcolonial About Archaeologies in Africa? In P. R. Schmidt (ed). *Postcolonial Archaeologies in Africa.* Santa Fe, NM: School for Advanced Research Press. pp. 1–20.

Segobye, A. K. (2009). Between Indigene and Citizen: Locating the Politics of the Past in Postcolonial Southern Africa. In P. R. Schmidt (ed). *Postcolonial Archaeologies in Africa.* Santa Fe, NM: School for Advanced Research Press, pp. 163–176.

Smith, L. (2007). *Decolonizing Methodologies: Research and Indigenous Peoples*. London: Zed Books Ltd.

Smith, L. J. (2006). *Uses of Heritage*. London and New York: Routledge.

Stroulia, Anna and Sutton Susan, B. (2009). Archaeological Sites and Local Places: Connecting the Dots. *Public Archaeology* 8 (2–3): 124–140.

Supernant, K. and Warrick, G. (2014). Challenges to Critical Community-Based Archaeological Practice in Canada. *Canadian Journal of Archaeology* 38: 563–591.

Taruvinga, P. and Ndoro, W. (2003). The Vandalism of the Domboshava Rock Painting Site, Zimbabwe: Some Reflections on Approaches to Heritage Management. *Conservation and Management of Archaeological Sites* 6 (1–1): 3–10.

Tunbridge, D. and Ashworth, G. (1996). *Dissonant Heritage*. Chichester: John Wiley and Sons.

Vilches, F., Christina, G., Ayala, P., and Ulises, C. (2015). The Contemporary Past of San Pedro de Atacama, Northern Chile: Public Archaeology? *Archaeologies: Journal of the World Archaeological Congress* 11 (3): 372–399.

Watson, S. (2007). Museums and Their Communities. In S. Watson (ed). *Museums and Their Communities*. London: Routledge, pp. 1–25.

Witcomb, A. (2007). A Place for All of Us? Museums and Communities. In S. Watson (ed). *Museums and Their Communities.* London: Routledge, pp. 133–157.

Witz, L. (2003). *Apartheid's Festival: Contesting South African National Pasts*. Bloomington, IN: Indian University Press.

Yerkovich, S. (2016). Ethics in a Changing Social Landscape. In B. L. Murphy (ed). *Museums, Ethics and Cultural Heritage.* London and New York: Routledge, pp. 242–250.

Zager, R. K. and Pluckhahn, T. J. (2013). Assessing Methodologies in Archaeological Ethnography: A Case for Incorporating Ethnographic Training in Graduate Archaeology Curricula. *Public Archaeology* 12 (1–1): 48–63.

Zimmerman, L. J. (2005). First, Be Humble: Working With Indigenous People and Other Descendant Communities. In C. Smith and H. M. Wobst (eds). *Indigenous Archaeologies: Decolonizing Theory and Practice*. London: Routledge, pp. 301–314.

4 Inclusion, collaboration and sustainable heritage conservation practices at the Ziwa archaeological site

Introduction

In this chapter, we will look at some of the challenges associated with disenfranchising communities in heritage conservation programmes (Chipangura et al. 2017). We will show how conflicts initially emerged at Ziwa as a consequence of a failure by Mutare Museum to recognize the importance of community participation and uses of the site. Ziwa archaeological site is located 20 km northwest of Nyanga Village on the lowlands of the northern part of the Eastern Highlands of Zimbabwe. The boundary of the site is marked by the Nyangombe River in the west and the Ziwa Mountain in the east. To the north and northwest the site shares a boundary with Matongo and Nyangare villages, respectively. Just like Matendera, this site is also under the administration of Mutare Museum. The cultural landscape derives its name from a prominent granite mountain on the southern boundary of the protected area. Ziwa is a representative sample of the Nyanga tradition which is constituted by an impressive landscape of stone-built features extending over more than 8,000 square kilometres (see Figure 4.1). The key archaeological elements of the cultural landscape comprise ancient stone terraces, stone enclosures, pit enclosures, hill forts and passages, smelting furnaces, grinding places, clearance cairns and other important remains constructed during the sixteenth and seventeenth centuries (Soper 2003).

The chapter highlights collaborative strategies adopted by the museum to deal with community conflict and conservation threats to the site. Out of this realisation, Mutare Museum embarked on a social inclusion project which entailed an active collaboration with the community in sustainable development programmes at Ziwa archaeological site. As argued in the ensuing chapters, collaborative strategies have to be at the centre of decolonial methodologies since they promote

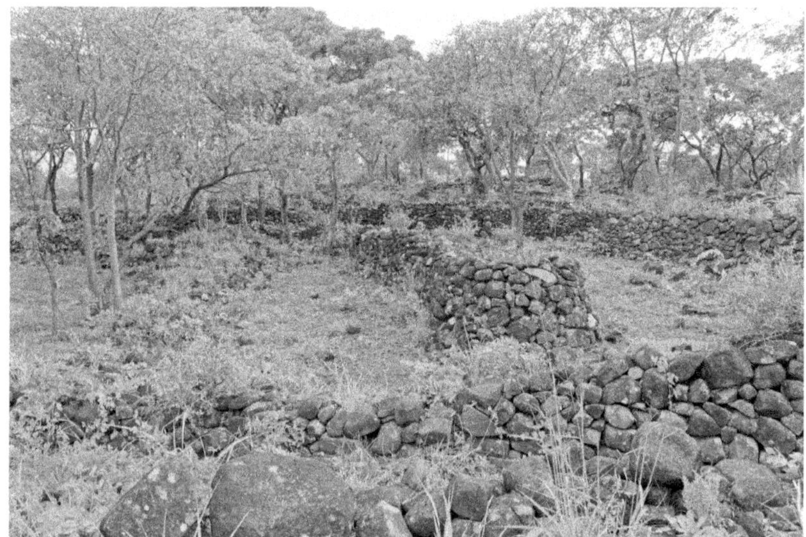

Figure 4.1 Ziwa archaeological site. Photograph by Njabulo Chipangura.

engagement over doctrine and multivocality over expert connoisseurship (Boast 2011). Collaboration have to ensure that communities are not considered as passive audiences for didactic and authoritative forms of knowledge production but are implicated in an ongoing process of knowledge production and debate as active co-producers (Butler and Lehrer 2016; Danbolt 2019; De Palma 2019; Hansen, Henningsen and Gregersen 2019). For this site, the museum chose a sustainable heritage conservation approach underscored by the recognition of everyday uses of the site by the community, and this paved way for collaborative heritage management. Sustainability in this case was encouraged through social cohesion and a sense of collective responsibility towards the utilization of cultural resources around Ziwa site.

Thinking beyond the Authorised Heritage Discourse

Smith's (2006) concept of Authorised Heritage Discourse (AHD) has provided a comprehensive treatise of how we can understand the ways in which official forms of heritage practices work. Importantly, she highlights how heritage in its tangible forms is a discourse that works within a range of socio-cultural practices, and that embedded in this discourse is a range of assumptions about the heritage's values linked and driven by aspects of monumentality and aesthetics (Smith 2006).

These processes elevate and foreground the authority of preservation institutions and experts through a set of practices and performances that populate expert constructions of heritage knowledge by obscuring the social and cultural practices that are the precursors to this materiality. Thus, AHD is a specific way in which heritage is managed which prioritises the perpetual conservation of qualities and characteristics connected to its intrinsic value (Ariese-Vandemeulebroucke 2018). It is the fascination, with the intrinsic material aspects of heritage places and objects, that has pitted institutions and experts against local communities all over the world (see Ndoro 2005) While many indigenous societies appreciate the physical structures associated with their cultural heritage, it is their sacredness and religious value that bring them closer to this heritage. For the local communities, heritage is thus fluid and intangible to a high degree and in their eyes should no longer be determined or controlled by experts but experienced and controlled by everyone (Russell 2010). Elsewhere it has been demonstrated that beyond the cultural aspects, local communities look at heritage places as spaces through which they can make claims around socioeconomic values and other forms of reparations (Shepherd 2008). This kind of understanding of heritage opens up a space for a plurality of meanings and values rather than one intrinsic value – one that erroneously only foregrounds the materiality of sites, objects and places. Therefore, we consider community uses of Ziwa and its cultural resources not only as a recognition of its intangible values, but also as a space through which the community addresses socio-economic issues. In dealing with the local communities at Ziwa, the museum had to be cognizant of the local values. The museum took approaches that challenged its own authority sites like Ziwa, moving away from its position as the "authorised" institution. For the museum, an effective way to do this was to acknowledge "traditional heritage management systems" by promoting practices derived from local communities that for decades had ensured the survival of this site. For the community, recourse to taboos, restrictions, rituals and sustainable use in the past were organic strategies used to preserve the site. In spite of the dominance of the institutional authoritative approaches to preservation, such practices had persisted among the local communities. Thus, instead of marginalizing the rituals as held in the local community, the museum's approach became that of creating productive synergies with the local leadership in the management and conservation of both tangible and intangible cultural heritage (Chipangura 2018).

The approaches adopted at Ziwa acknowledged the fact that heritage conservation is a multifaceted concept which involves looking after both the tangible and intangible aspects of a cultural landscape by highlighting the attachments which individuals and groups of people have within its location. Smith (2006) posits heritage as a "… cultural practice involving the construction and regulation of a range of values and understandings." Such values and understandings tend to vary between different groups of people and fundamentally also determine the ways in which heritage is conserved and managed. Previously, at Ziwa differences existed between Mutare Museum and the community which emanated from an overemphasis of scientific conservation ethos by the former at the expense of socio-cultural values. Community members were randomly cutting trees down inside the vast site as they protested against their exclusion from decision making (Chipangura 2018). Cutting down trees at Ziwa posed conservation challenges because most trees cut were within the archaeological site. However, the community argued that their forefathers used the site freely since time immemorial, and as a result the site has survived to this day. They considered that cutting down trees was a conservation function aimed at clearing overgrown vegetation on the ancient terraced walls (Chipangura et al. 2017).

A solution to the conflict was the integration of community members in the conservation of this site through collaborative approaches. The approach acknowledges that community knowledge inherited from previous generations is useful because it informs contemporary heritage practices and how people relate with heritage places (National Heritage Act 2016: National Museums and Monuments of Zimbabwe Act 2001). It acknowledges and promotes popular knowledge, collective memory, rituals and other cultural manifestations as essential components that have ensured the survival of cultural sites for years. However, even in such collaborative scenarios it becomes essential to acknowledge that heritage communities are not homogenous, because different people usually have different opinions on how they should be involved in managing the heritage and hence new forms of conflict could emerge. Academics and heritage practitioners have highlighted how the notion of community itself can be so vague as to lose all meaning because it is laden with multifarious definitions and that the different uses of heritage and its importance to different people in a community makes it inevitable that it can be a major arena of conflict and contestation (Graham 2005). However, effective collaboration with societies entails not only acknowledging the fact of ever-persistent conflicts, but also knowing how to effectively work productively with the conflicting groups. Although differences initially existed between Ziwa community and Mutare Museum, a shared responsibility later emerged in which both tangible and intangible aspects of the heritage are now being looked after through an integration of scientific and traditional management models. Community participation in heritage activities was used as the yardstick that paved the way for cooperation between the heritage authorities and communities.

Community participation in the crafting of the Ziwa by-laws

Involving communities in the management of Ziwa is a process that facilitated its conservation and sustainable use. An important aspect of the strategy was to acknowledge the spiritual values ascribed to the site by local communities. The significance of this site to the community can be deduced from the values that they attach entrenched in terms of spiritual and symbolic associations (Meskelll 2009). It is because of its significance that the community still uses the site for various rituals that have been upheld since time immemorial. These living traditions and rituals function as important aspects of heritage conservation because the community treats the site as a living heritage – a sacred space to be revered, respected and protected by the community. At Ziwa, the *Matumba* site has always been used by the community to perform rainmaking ceremonies – a sacred practice which has survived the test of time and the threats of modernity. This annual ritual practice has not compromised the structural survival of the stone walls over the years (Chipangura 2014, 2015). Some elderly members of the community prepare a traditional beer brew for twenty-one days in the month of October each year. The beer is then sprinkled around the stone wall and at a nearby rock painting during the rituals which are associated with petitioning rains. It is through these practices that local communities participate in the production of meaning at the sites, allowing for the articulation, foregrounding and promotion of local ways of knowing and cultural practices accords a holistic interpretation of the site. By allowing and facilitating these practices, the museum establishes a sense of ownership among the community, according to the cultural agency, while at the same time giving the community the agency and authority to ensure the protection and preservation of the site (Manyanga 2001).

While for many years, the ritual aspects of the site had not been emphasised by the museum management, local communities have always laid claim to these sites as their shrines (Pwiti and Mvenge 1996; Taruvinga and Ndoro 2003; Ndoro 2005; Fontein 2006). Recognising that Ziwa is still a living and revered cultural site embedded with spiritual and symbolic values enabled Mutare Museum to rethink the whole process of heritage protection and management and reframe the approaches to working with local communities. The museum respected the fact that these cultural practices had been undertaken at the site even before the advent of scientific heritage management systems which prioritises tangibility and monumentality over the intangible aspects of the site. These official management systems, introduced around 1890, soon after the colonisation of Zimbabwe by the British, disrupted existing pragmatic traditional management systems that to a large extent allowed some change, at the same time preserving certain core values and the essence of social identity. The earliest forms of protection were ushered in with the passing of a suite of legislation between 1902 and 1972. These included the Ancient Monuments Protection Ordinance in 1902 which was enacted mainly to protect Zimbabwe sites against vandalism by treasure hunters, where "ancient monuments and relics" were defined as any material predating 1800.[1] The Bushmen Relics Ordinance of 1912 was passed to protect rock art sites. This ordinance was influenced by large scale exploitation of rock art sites.[2] These were followed by the National Monuments Act of 1932 and the 1972 National Museum and Monuments Act, both of which expanded the types of sites protected while nationalizing all important archaeological and historic sites. What is key to note is how these legal instruments emphasized the protection of the physical integrity of sites. The ordinances did not recognise the ritual uses of the sites by local communities, and the use of a lot of the sites for rituals and other practices by local communities was completely outlawed (Chirikure and Pwiti 2008)

This is the context within which most preservation practices at Ziwa had been implemented, yet one can acknowledge that these longstanding ritual practices at sites like Ziwa occupied an important biography of the sites and provided a link with the local communities. Thus, before the heritage became physically tangible at Ziwa, there were intangible ideas related to spirituality, symbolism and beliefs of the people that were the precursors to monumentality. These are the same ideas that have been transmitted today and resonate with the rain-making rituals described above. To recognise the importance of intangible heritage at Ziwa, the National Museums and Monuments of Zimbabwe Act (NMMZ) allows the use of the site by community members without hindrance. Social value is not about the past or about social history, but about people's attachment to places in the present (Davison 2000). Values are therefore a product of society, which is why Jokiletho (2007) argues that the identification of heritage and its safeguarding fundamentally depends on the awareness of values and significance. The attachment of values within Ziwa by the heritage community is drawn from the socio-cultural use of the site during ritual ceremonies associated with rain-making. To them monumentality is a function of the rituals in which they argue that the stone structures were constructed as protected cultural precincts where ritual activities were undertaken.

In many ways, this acknowledgement of the mystical, religious and divine and acknowledgement of local practices becomes central on movement towards decolonial museums that operate in what Nick Shepherd and Anton Haber frame as "the Post-disciplinary Worlds," which deal with the lines of tension between the disciplinary (in our case museum knowledge and representation) forms of practice and rival knowledge regimes (Shepherd and Haber 2014: 6). Through this acknowledgement, and working with the practices, performances and articulations of the spirit related to objects, sites and places, we can perhaps imagine a decolonial museology that begins to effectively challenge the hegemony of disciplinary and Western epistemologies.

Mutare Museum and communities: resolving conflict at Ziwa

Mutare Museum and local villagers were at loggerheads with regard to the exploitation of resources in this Ziwa cultural landscape which covers over eight thousand square kilometres. Since Ziwa is located around villages, which use firewood, it became inevitable that they would rely on firewood as a source of energy. Consequently, security guards at Ziwa were always involved in running battles with villagers whom they accused of "stealing" firewood. The contestation between Mutare Museum and villagers revolved around two parallel aspects that had a completely different bearing on each party. For the Mutare Museum, the continuous and random cutting down of trees at Ziwa was posing a serious conservation challenge because most of the firewood was being harvested from the terraced walls. As a result, the number of terraced walls which were collapsing was high.

In addition, since Mutare Museum has the legal mandate to manage the site, villagers caught on the site were liable to face prosecution for trespassing and stealing. The legal mandate is derived from the NMMZ Act (2001),[3] which gives the institution the power to protect, preserve and present all national monuments in the country.[4] Meanwhile, whereas Mutare Museum had a legal basis to manage the site, the villagers were arguing that their forefathers have been using the site since time immemorial without any restrictions imposed on them, and as a result the site itself has managed to survive up to this day.[5] Thus, they were of the opinion that traditional management systems that were in place in the past must be recognised and work hand in hand with enacted laws. To the local populace, cutting down of trees for firewood was therefore not regarded as "stealing" but rather a conservation measure that would ensure that the walls are not affected by overgrowing trees. This practice was deemed by the villagers as having contributed to the wellbeing of this site; stopping it was akin to putting an end to a living traditional conservation practice.[6]

However, because of simmering conflicts in resource utilisation, Mutare Museum saw fit to draft some by-laws – the Ziwa by-laws Statutory Instrument 143 of 2011 (NMMZ 2011). Therefore, the Ziwa by-laws were crafted as general regulations to guide the exploitation of firewood within the site by members of the community. Effectively the by-laws were passed to allow heritage communities to be involved in the management of this site in a sustainable way. A consultative meeting was carried out with the community before the by-laws were adopted. The by-laws were prepared to designate the utilisation of resources at Ziwa by villagers in a sustainable way that would not compromise the conservation of the site. Among other things, the by-laws also spelled out Mutare Museum's legal mandate in the management of the site, while at the same time, importantly, recognised the day-to-day use of the site by the villagers.[7] From the presentation, which was debated and later adopted in consensus with the villagers who attended the meeting, it was agreed that households would be given at most three days each month to cut firewood within designated areas of the monument. This was born out of the realisation that a total ban on the exploitation of firewood was not an option as it continuously created tensions which were leading to conservation conflicts between Mutare Museum and the local community. The local community relies on firewood, thatching grass, poles and grazing from the Ziwa cultural landscape; consequently, uncontrolled exploitation of these resources would also cause environmental degradation as well as destroy archaeological structures. According to the by-laws, an application in writing was to be submitted to the site administrator who would then show the villagers the areas on which to cut down the firewood.[8]

In addition to this, the by-laws made a provision to allow monitored cattle grazing within designated sections of the site.[9] Villagers could let their cattle graze inside the vast monument when there was somebody monitoring the movement of the herd so that it would not disturb the terraced walls and other stone structures. The use of the site for various ritual ceremonies by the traditional leadership of this community was also upheld in the by-laws. However, the other community subsistence operations closely tied to the conservation of the site, such as hunting of game animals, were completely outlawed and prohibited.[10]

Out of all these tensions, negotiations, compromises and subsequent agreement in part, it is worth recognising that villagers are important heritage communities which must not be side-lined. By way of inclusive management involving community participation, as was provided for in the by-laws, Mutare Museum managed to alleviate the previous tensions that affected the site and affected social change. There was a commitment to support communities living adjacent to Ziwa so as to avert further degradation and obliteration of the cultural landscape whose intangible cultural practices were considered vital since Ziwa is a living site (NMMZ 1992, 2013, 2016).

Museums as social agents: the Ziwa Beekeeping Project and community development

Another project that was self-initiated by the villagers at Ziwa as a sustainable way of managing their cultural resources was a beekeeping project, which was in turn overwhelmingly supported by Mutare Museum. The project is now producing honey for consumption and for sale on the local market. In the project, local community members were trained by Mutare Museum in various beekeeping techniques. They were also provided with free material to make beehives which they could install anywhere within the vast site. This project empowered the heritage community by allowing them to generate their own income from selling honey which subsequently curtailed the over-exploitation of resources in the monument. Most importantly, this initiative brought about a degree of realisation and resolve among members of the community on the need to sustainably manage the monument and its associated resources (Chiwaura and Chabata 2007a). In addition, through its implementation it improved heritage management and conservation in the area by raising consciousness to halt deforestation. As a result, there has been a marked change of attitude of the local community towards trees in and around Ziwa. The cutting down of trees and the occurrence of fires has been greatly reduced. Overall, the Ziwa Beekeeping Project is empowering communities and has become a model for sustainable cultural heritage management for replication in Zimbabwe and probably more generally in Africa (Chiwaura and Chabata 2007b)

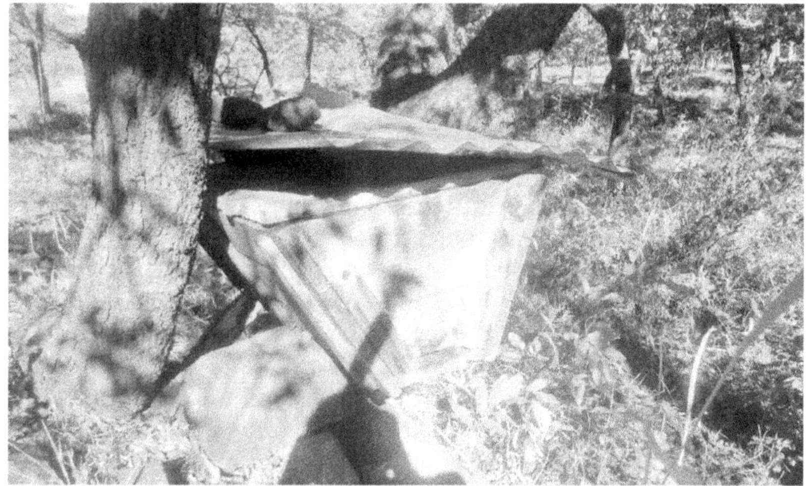

Figure 4.2 Ziwa Beekeeping Project. Photograph by Njabulo Chipangura.

Another potential initiative that would also aid the sustainable utilisation of resources around Ziwa would be the establishment of woodlots of both indigenous and exotic trees in the surrounding communities which will regenerate vegetation for firewood and timber. The firewood and timber can also be sold, thus becoming income-generating projects for the locals. The proposed woodlot establishment is a medium- to long-term strategy that would reduce exploitation pressure on this cultural landscape. In recognition of the importance of Ziwa cultural landscape, Mutare Museum, local communities and the Agricultural Extension Service also conduct an annual agricultural show at the site. During the show, members of the local community exhibit their farming produce in a competition (Chiwaura and Chabata 2007b). The show has enabled Mutare Museum to market its activities and, more importantly, succeeded in making the local communities conscious of the need to respect and sustainably conserve their cultural and natural heritage in the Ziwa cultural landscape. This practice also highlights the importance of the site as a prehistoric agricultural landscape among members of the local community.

Conclusion

The activities at the Ziwa site demonstrate key issues. One is the ever-persistent debates about how communities get involved in decision making about important heritage sites within their locales. For

NMMZ its role was that of a broker, rather than a powerful state agency. Here the ways of engagement included the involvement of local political authorities and the traditional power structures, in an inclusive engagement about setting rules and by-laws on how to use sites. The second aspect is that of how communities can benefit economically from the sites in their areas. During the colonial era such sites were cordoned off with local communities displaced by state-run entities for the purpose of preservation, research and tourism. In the postcolonial era, such sites had to be reimagined as central to local communities' sense of identity and socio-economic wellbeing. Museums and preservation organizations need to look beyond the imperatives of preservation and conservation and draw from local practices and economic activities to confer spaces for the sites to be optimally used in local economic beneficiation. A sense of ownership is cultivated, and in the process enhances the preservation and protection of sites by local communities.

Notes

1 The Ancient Monuments of Rhodesia Ordinance of 1902 was one of the earliest state efforts to regulate the activities and protect sites from destruction was the 1902 Ordinance, a legislative order that was meant to protect archaeological monuments. The 1902 ordinance aptly named the "Better Protection of Ancient Monuments and Ancient Relics Ordinance," sought to improve the protection of monuments from further damage by colonial treasure hunters
2 The Rhodesia Bushmen Relics Ordinance of 1912 followed the 1902 ordinance and entrenched formal protection of archaeological and rock art sites.
3 It is important to note that the National Museums and Monuments of Zimbabwe (NMMZ) Act, which governs the operations of all museums has been reviewed and will be amended into The National Heritage Act of Zimbabwe. Community participation is one of the most important inclusions in the forthcoming act which will be called the National Heritage Act of Zimbabwe. Public and stakeholder consultations during the drafting of the new act were carried out throughout the country between 2013 and 2016.
4 The National Museums and Monuments of Zimbabwe Act Chapter 25:11 of 2001. This Act was amended from the 1972 National Museums and Monuments Act 25:11 which ushered in a key change to the way museums and heritage sites were managed in Rhodesia. It is this Act which combined and linked the management of all designated national heritage sites within specific museums. As per this Act, the regulation of museums, national monuments and archaeological sites which were previously managed by two separate state-supported organisations: the National Museums of Rhodesia and the National Monuments Commission were

amalgamated into the National Museums and Monuments of Rhodesia (NMMR). The Act consolidated the two departments creating a unified legal institutional structure for museums and monuments. This link between museums and monuments/sites has survived to the present.

5 Interview with Headman Saunyama on 11 October 2013.
6 Interview with Headman Saunyama on 11 October 2013.
7 Ziwa by-laws Statutory Instrument 143 of 2011, National Museums and Monuments of Zimbabwe.
8 Ziwa by-laws Statutory Instrument 143 of 2011, National Museums and Monuments of Zimbabwe.
9 Ziwa by-laws Statutory Instrument 143 of 2011, National Museums and Monuments of Zimbabwe.
10 Ziwa by-laws Statutory Instrument 143 of 2011, National Museums and Monuments of Zimbabwe.

Bibliography

Ariese-Vandemeulebroucke, C. (2018). *The Social Museum in the Caribbean: Grassroots Heritage Initiatives and Community Engagement*. Leiden, The Netherlands: Sidestone Press.

Boast, R. (2011). Neocolonial Collaboration: Museum as Contact Zone Revisited. *Museum Anthropology* 56 (1): 65–70.

Bruchac, M. (2014). Decolonization in Archaeological Theory. In C. Smith. *Encyclopaedia of Global Archaeology*. New York: Springer, pp. 2069–2077.

Butler, S. and Lehrer, E. (2016). Introduction: Curatorial Dreaming. In S. R. Butler and E. Lehrer (eds). *Curatorial Dreams*. London: McGill-Queen's University Press, pp. 3–26.

Chipangura, N. (2014). Rethinking the Practice of Collecting and Displaying Ethnographic Objects at Mutare Museum. In R. Omar (ed). *Museums and the Idea of Historical Progress*. Cape Town: Iziko Museums Publications, pp. 178–190.

Chipangura, N. (2015). Representation, Reproduction and Transmission of Public Culture in Zimbabwean Museums, Commemorations and festivals. In M. Mawere et al. (eds). *African Museums in the Making: Reflections on the Politics of Material and Public Culture in Zimbabwe*. Bamenda: Langaa Publishers.

Chipangura, N. (2018). Cultural Heritage Sites and Contemporary Uses; Finding a Balance between Monumentality and Intangibility in Eastern Zimbabwe. In C. Waelde, C. Cummings, M. Pavis and H. Enright (eds). *Research Handbook on Contemporary Intangible Cultural Heritage Law and Heritage*. Cheltenham: Edward Elgar Publishing, pp. 379–398.

Chipangura, N., Chiripanhura, P. and Nyamagodo, S. (2017). Policy Formulation and Collaborative Management: The Case of Ziwa Site, Eastern Zimbabwe. *Museum International* 69 (275–267): 116–123.

Chirikure, S. and Pwiti, G. (2008). Community Involvement in Archaeology and Cultural Heritage Management: An Assessment from Case Studies in Southern Africa and Elsewhere. *Current Anthropology* 49 (3).

Chiwaura, H. and Chabata, F. (2007a). An Evaluation of the Ziwa Beekeeping Project. Unpublished report. Harare: National Museums and Monuments of Zimbabwe.

Chiwaura, H. and Chabata, F. (2007b). An Evaluation of the Agricultural Show. Unpublished report. Harare: National Museums and Monuments of Zimbabwe.

Danbolt, M. (2019). Exhibition Addresses: The Production of Publics in Exhibitions on Colonial History. In M. V. Hansen, A. F. Henningsen and A. Gregersen (eds). *Curatorial Challenges: Interdisciplinary Perspectives on Contemporary Curating*. London: Routledge, pp. 65–79.

Davison, G. (2000). *The Use and Abuse of Australian History*. Australia: Allen & Unwin Book Publishers.

Delafons, J. J. (1997). *Politics and Preservation: A Policy History of the Built Heritage 1882–1996.* Routledge.

De Palma, M. (2019). Selfies, Yoga and Hip Hop: Expanding the Roles of Museums. In V. Golding and J. Walklate (eds). *Museums and Communities: Diversity, Dialogue and Collaborations in an Age of Migrations*. Cambridge: Cambridge Scholars Publishing, pp. 230–259.

Fontein, J. (2006). *The Silence of Great Zimbabwe: Contested Landscapes and the Power of Heritage*. Harare: Weaver Press.

Hansen, M. Henningsen, A. and Gregersen, A. (2019). "Introduction." In by M. Hansen, A. Henningsen and A. Gregersen (eds). *Curatorial Challenges: Interdisciplinary Perspectives on Contemporary Curating*. London: Routledge, pp. 1–6.

Manyanga, M. (2001). Intangible Cultural Heritage and the Empowerment of Local Communities. Paper presented at the ICOMOS Conference on Intangible Heritage, Victoria Falls, Zimbabwe.

Meskell, L. (2009). *Cosmopolitan Archaeologies*. Durham, NC: Duke University Press.

Ndoro, W. (2005). *The Preservation of Great Zimbabwe: Your Monuments Our Shrine*. Rome: ICCROM.

NMMZ. (2011). *Ziwa By-Laws, Statutory Instrument 143 of 2011*. Harare: National Museums and Monuments of Zimbabwe.

NMMZ. (2013). *Matendera Festival Concept Paper*. Harare: National Museums and Monuments of Zimbabwe.

NMMZ. (2016). Matendera National Monument File. Accessed at Mutare Museum on 17.11.16.

NMMZ. (1992). *Great Zimbabwe Management Plan*. Harare: National Museums and Monuments of Zimbabwe.

Pwiti, G. and Mvenge, G. (1996). Archaeologists, Tourists, and Rainmakers: Problems in the Management of Rock Art Sites in Zimbabwe, a Case Study of Domboshava National Monument. In G. Pwiti and R. Soper (eds). *Aspects of African Archaeology: Papers from the 10th Congress of the Pan-African Association for Prehistory and Related Studies*. Harare: University of Zimbabwe Publications, pp. 817–824.

Rowntree, L. B. and Conkey, M. W. (1980). Symbolism and the Cultural Landscape. *Annals of the Association of American Geographers* 70 (4): 459–474.

Shepherd, N. (2008). Heritage. In N. Shepherd and S. Robins (eds). *New South African Keywords.* Johannesburg: Jacana Media, pp. 116–128.

Shepherd, N. and Haber, A. (2014). *After Ethics: Ancestral Voices and Postdisciplinary Worlds in Archaeology*. New York, NY: Springer Press.

Smith, L. J. (2006). *Uses of Heritage.* London: Routledge.

Soper, R. (2003) *Nyanga: Ancient Fields, Settlements and Agricultural History in Zimbabwe. British Institute in Eastern Africa Memoir*. Nairobi: British Institute in Eastern Africa.

Taruvinga, P. and Ndoro, W. (2003). The Vandalism of the Domboshava Rock Painting Site, Zimbabwe: Some Reflections on Approaches to Heritage Management. *Conservation and Management of Archaeological Sites* 6 (1–1): 3–10.

The National Heritage Act of Zimbabwe Draft of February 2016.

The National Museums and Monuments of Zimbabwe Act Chapter 25:11 of 2001.

Conclusion

Local communities and the future of the African museum

Dealing with the past

African museums were established during the colonial era, where they served narrow interests and audiences. Their practices of collection, classification, containment and representation were influenced by biased knowledge practices of the period. This book comes at a time when there are debates on how decoloniality can be empirically approached within the African museum practice. Proposals have been made to reconfigure the museum practice which in many Africa countries is still rooted in western paradigms and conceptions of thought. Several strategies have been proffered to enhance the role of museums and communities in Africa or to assist museums in facing new challenges in twenty-first century Africa (Abungu L. 2005; Abungu G. 2001, 2002, 2006). The foregrounding of the emerging strategies and practices around the continent is key in articulating and demonstrating the operationalisation of this desire for change in the ground. Here, we have demonstrated how a small museum in Eastern Zimbabwe has over the past decade been on the forefront of spearheading decolonial projects that are undergirded by community collaborations, inclusivity, critical dialogue and multivocality methodologies which are challenging ills and bad legacies of the colonisation. Thus, we have presented it in the book as an important intervention for the African museum practice which has been grappling with how to deal with objects and displays structure by colonial system of classification and separated from communities of origin. While the museum during the colonial era, through its collection practices, modes of classification, categorisation and naming, subjected African cultures and communities to a colonial gaze, one that satisfied scientific priorities and social curiosities, the current museum looks beyond its own structures and trajectories of power to collect, represent or classify, to allow space for communities outside the museum and to democratically participate in activities that serve local values, interests and challenges (Sandahl 2019).

These ways of working have put the museum on a trajectory to deconstruct, challenge and unsettle its colonial past and move towards the museum being a decolonial site that centres local communities, practices and aspirations above scientific or expert agendas. In essence, decolonial initiatives that formed the core argument of this book were premised on self-representation where previously marginalised community knowledge challenged colonially derived curatorial practices. In light of these arguments, it is paramount to acknowledge that from an African point of view when objects were placed in museums they were robbed of their original symbolic meanings and incorporated into new frameworks of significance arranged according to new principles of materiality, authenticity and analogy. At the same time, it must also be acknowledged that these objects were not created in vacuum as their meanings are often interwoven with words, proverbs, song and dance and cannot be separated from these underlying elements. Linked to this, another overarching argument that radiates throughout the book is the idea of looking at ethnographic objects in museums not only as physical things but also in the people, changing practices and belief systems that lend them meaning. This view is echoed by Abungu (2019: 64) who argues that "there is need for a paradigm shift that will see the museum definition and museum responsibilities take into cognisance not only a linear material first approach but a multi-variant people centred approach ..." Henceforth, collaborations as a decolonial strategy can transform ethnographic museums from being places that were once regarded as displaying "others" to locations of cultural revitalisation, community voice and empowerment (Onciul 2019). In our case studies in the book, we also illustrated how accepting source communities as experts and research partners has changed the museum practice by opening up different ways of knowing and caring for the past.

Broadly, the African museum of the future is one that should embrace the potency of objects as living beings which indigenous communities can touch, smell and taste. These objects constitute a part of an interconnected whole, which means that the superficial binary division between tangible and intangible does not exist. Although these objects may appear mundane in colonial ethnographic classifications, they have individual biographies and carry with them important meanings connected to ritual and cultural functions located in societies of origin. We illustrated this by discussing a new exhibition at Mutare Museum which was co-curated with the community by reconfiguring Shona traditional drums in the old Beit Gallery. Ritual uses of contemporary drums by communities in Eastern Zimbabwe provided us with a much deeper understanding of the silent biographies of similar drums that were appropriated and dumped in museum during the colonial period. Therefore, conscious of old colonial museological practices that were driven by the ethnographic gaze and scientific inquiries, Mutare Museum embraced new museology and co-curatorship as decolonial strategies in reorganising these traditional drums in the Beit Gallery. These concepts allowed for collaboration with the local community in the reinterpretation of meaning and uses of the drums. A new interactive exhibition was born out of this collaborative exercise, and we have argued that such a practice is one of the ways in which the colonial frame of a museum can be dismantled, thereby opening up for multivocality derived from everyday experiences of communities. Therefore, it is important to recognise that traditional drums were not just static ethnographic objects displayed for the sole purpose of the visual gaze. This is because before they were disentangled from their original context, they were used in various ritual processes. Practically, the use of collaborative techniques in the making of this exhibition can be regarded as part and parcel of a methodological approach that was embraced in the decolonisation of the museum practice. While allowing for more comprehensive interpretation of the ethnographic material culture, by infusing life, the activities accorded the participation of previously marginalised stakeholders back into the museum, deconstructing the institution's own normative curatorial processes. The museum opens itself to different ways of collating, categorisation or classification, allowing the knowledge from the local communities to take central stage in museum knowledge production and representation.

Social activism and post-museum: looking beyond the walls

Developments in Africa have shown how museums, in the postcolonial context, can engage in processes of transformation and change relative effectiveness. Selected museum projects in South Africa such as the District Six project in Cape Town, and numerous other museum development projects after 1994, have shown the world how museums can engage with wider, previously marginalised communities, contribute to restitution, social transformation, community self-representation and rehumanisation of African societies and cultures (see Coombes 2003; Corsane 2004; Davison 2005; Rassool 2006; 2015,

2018). Commendable as these developments have been, except for a few cases, the focus has largely been on looking at museums in their normative configurations of institutions that engage in preservation and representation of histories, societies or cultures, mostly located in urban metropoles. There is still a lot to be said and explored on how museums can extend this reach much further. It is clear that museums have to look beyond their four walls and beyond their immediate locales by moving into sites and places outside of the centralised metropoles and engaging with communities spread around the museums. The administrative structure of museums in Zimbabwe, where museums in regions are also mandated with managing other archaeological and heritage sites, has been an opportunity for effective engagement and working with local communities. The approach of taking a social activist stance to issues facing contemporary societies is an efficient way to embed the museum within its local communities. Beyond the usual museum practices of collection, research or knowledge production and exhibition, a museum in sync with topical issues is one in sync with its stakeholders. Sites outside the museum allow local communities to participate in fulfilling self-presentation and allow them to write their cultural and contemporary shelves in the public sphere, provided by and abrogated by a once colonial museum. As the museum deals with and deconstructs this colonial past, it simultaneously becomes a site for community engagement and social activism, contributing to addressing social justice.

The decolonial initiatives discussed in this book came out of the *Ngoda: The Wealth Beneath Our Feet* exhibition which was curated by the Mutare Museum in collaboration with villagers from Chiadzwa. Prior to this decolonised exhibition, this museum was regarded as a building that housed old objects of the past and was irrelevant to the everyday struggles of the community which it served. However, through collaborative researching, designing and production of this exhibition, the museum managed to effect social change. Surface diamonds were discovered in Chiadzwa, Eastern Zimbabwe in 2006 by community members before they were displaced and relocated to Arda Transau in 2008. This became a topical hot-spot issue which we decided to portray in an exhibition, and in the process the museum became an active space of critical public pedagogy and an agent for social change. As we were carrying out the research for this exhibition, villagers expressed a plethora of challenges that they were facing that emanated from the discovery of diamonds in the area. The diamond as presented by the community became an object of social inequality, and instead of uplifting their standards of living it further impoverished them. Displacements to pave way for formal diamond mining resulted in Chiadzwa villagers being given small pieces of land at Arda Farm where they were relocated to. Villagers shared bitter stories of their daily struggles and called upon the government to address them. The exhibition therefore provided a contact zone in which the affected community aired out their grievances that eventually captured the attention of the government. Being an important public pedagogy institution, Mutare Museum beamed video and audio recordings on a wall projector narrating the challenges that were being faced by the villagers. By critically engaging with communities and addressing their daily struggles in an exhibition, Mutare Museum became an agent for social change. This therefore implies that although the museum practice in Africa was shaped by colonialism, by engaging in social activities and speaking for the rights of communities in exhibitions, the museum can become a relevant social-inclusion platform. In light of this observation, Sandell (2007: 96) argues that "museums can impact positively on the lives of disadvantaged or marginalised individuals, act as a catalyst for social regeneration and as a vehicle for empowerment with specific communities and also contribute towards the creation of more equitable societies."

In the book we have also argued that the Matendera festival which is hosted by Mutare Museum is a form of intangible cultural heritage practice that collaboratively engages communities in producing insightful narratives on the meaning of the archaeological site previously thought to be an exclusive domain of heritage experts. Activities discussed which constitute intangible expressions by the community anchored around the festival include traditional dances, music, poetry, social games, a marathon and the preparation of traditional dishes. By partaking in these activities at the site, the Matendera community was endowed with a sense of belonging and shared entitlement in the production of heritage knowledge. Therefore, the festival allowed them to speak and write their own narratives drawn from their local understanding of the site and underwritten by intangible practices which have been passed from generation to generation. Meanwhile, at Ziwa, Mutare Museum has also been working with communities in sustainable heritage conservation projects that are providing them with a source of livelihood. In this regard, we looked at how the Ziwa Bee Keeping Project was formulated as one such project where communities are actively involved. Heritage conflicts were also mitigated at the site through collaborative management in which by-laws were designed to allow for sustainable use of resources at Ziwa site. The by-laws as a policy were developed by Mutare Museum in collaboration with the local community. The precursor to policy formulation at this site was the growing tension on resource utilisation between the heritage community and the museum. Therefore, by adopting the Ziwa by-laws as the principal policy, a mutually constituted cooperation was born that subsequently paved the way for an inclusive heritage management model. Through the implementation of this policy, harvesting of firewood by community members at the site was decriminalized. This was attained by putting in place a monitored control mechanism which provided a win-win situation for the previously warring parties.

Working with communities: collaboration and inherited practices

We have argued throughout this book that collaborations can potentially transform African museums from being places that were once regarded as displaying "others" to locations of cultural revitalisation, community voice and empowerment (Onciul 2019: 160). Consequently, accepting source communities as experts and research partners can change museum practice by opening up different ways of knowing and caring for the past (Onciul 2019). Questions must be asked about the nature of communities and the various ways in which museums can engage with them. Museum practices are influenced by various political and power imperatives, and museums themselves have always been purveyors of lopsided power relationships in community engagement, where the power of the museum – both as an institution and in its authorised curatorial practices – marginalises local communities (Hooper-Greenhill 2007; Bennett 1995). However, De Parma (2019: 249) argues that collaborative programmes can transform museums from being cemeteries of dead objects lying behind glass into active places where culture is performed through participation of the whole community. Collaborative approaches decentre the authority of museum curators by allowing for an investigative process in which decision making about knowledge and objects of the past is a shared responsibility (Chipangura 2019; Onciul 2019). Diverse perspectives emerge in the interpretation and presentation of objects in the exhibition informed by indigenous ontologies and epistemologies with more than one significance, origin and/or use (Vilches et al. 2015). A decolonising approach that is undergirded by collaborations and community-driven curatorship gives agency to indigenous communities that are able to decide how they want stories to be told in museum exhibitions. In light of this, working with communities in the making of exhibitions presents opportunities for a shared engagement with plural voices incorporated into the narrative. Therefore, the old colonial practice that once defined museums in their predominant control of mediation, contextualisation and interpretation of objects, with curators regarded as authorised "keepers," has gradually been coming under scrutiny. This is because the museum is now redefined as an open public space that addresses contentious issues within community settings.

Exhibition designing has become more collaborative, with an emphasis on co-curatorship which is replacing the former anonymous, institutional monolingual power with multiple voices from communities that adhere to different versions of the past. The new planning, presentation and interpretive methods used in such exhibitions enable communities to become actively involved in self-representation or in critiques of cultural, economic or ideological impositions that affect them. In this process, museum curators become facilitators and not undisputable champions with authorised knowledge. Curatorship has thus evolved from being a strict, specialised connoisseurship of individuals to a public service that attends to problems in contemporary communities (Schorch, McCarthy and Durr 2019). Hence, communities are valuable sources of expertise and partners in knowledge creation, and not passive recipients of authorised discourses. The communities no longer just enjoy museum products, but also actively direct the activities of museums (Pham 2019). This collaborative approach to exhibition production is reflective of shared authority between the community and museum curators. Exhibitions have become more than just sites for the manifestation of preconceived curatorial theory but are increasingly sites of collaborative research and knowledge production (Butler and Lehrer 2016). They have shifted from the status of merely presenting concluded results into important active venues for analysing social issues and producing relevant knowledge (Bjerregaard 2019; Dahre 2019; Hansen, Henningsen and Gregersen, 2019).

Collaborative approaches give room for more participatory and co-curated exhibition-making practices. A collaborative methodology in a museum has been described by Shelton (2018) as encompassing three elements:

> transforming the role of a curator into a facilitator in which the community independently takes charge and determines the subject of an exhibition; collaboration in periodic dialogues with the community to ensure the fidelity of the exhibition with their expectations; and collaboration as a dialogic process through which culture is generated in conversations between curators and the community representatives (Shelton 2018: xviii).

Simon (2010) also describes collaborations as fulfilling the mandate of what she calls participatory museums, which is different from traditional museums in that it involves stakeholders and is central to cultural and community life. The concept of participatory museum can be closely linked to Clifford's (2007) and Pratt's (1992) concept of the contact zone, which is a force for inclusionist collaboration programs and the development of mutual interests with all social groups (Boast 2011; Walklate 2018; Dahre 2019). However, it has been argued that contact zones are merely neo-colonial sites in which hierarchies of power are still present because asymmetric relationships exist between museum "experts" and community members (Boast 2011). A critique of the collaboration process is usually around the location of power in these activities (La Salle 2010; Golding and Walklate 2019). It is for this reason that Boast (2011: 58) argues that no matter how much we might think of pluralizing knowledge production in museums through collaborations, the intellectual control will still remain vested in the hands of curators. Therefore, even though community collaboration has become a major museum decolonising methodology, there is no critical evaluation of what it means in terms of geographies of power (Shelton 2018).

Museums, decolonised knowledge and epistemic justice

One of the most pressing and urgent issues facing museums in post-colonial Africa is how to embrace local communities from whom a lot of the material culture in the museums was collected, sometimes through unethical and violent means. As knowledge institutions, museums have a moral obligation to integrate local knowledge that has been related to the margins of cultural representation and to the fringes of knowledge production. The engagement activities highlighted in the preceding chapters talk to interesting relationships between museums, experts and local communities in self representation and in processes of knowledge production. The practices unsettle the museum versus local community, or the expert-non-expert dichotomy in the process of representation and knowledge production. The museum space – itself regarded as a product of colonial knowledge practices where marginalised traditional objects were stored – can be used to confer new forms of engagement where source communities are allowed entrance into the museum, not as subjects to be represented, but as equal players in the curatorial processes (Sweet and Kelly 2019). This work with communities challenges the museum's troubled past, while giving local communities space to self-represent and to change the nature of knowledge in the museum (Clifford 2007). This highlights how museums have enabled a new trajectory for expert-community relations and engendered new curatorial approaches that take local communities as partners. For many African museums burdened with collections uprooted from communities during the colonial era, these new approaches should reframe museum practice and facilitate self-representation, where space is given to local people so that they can challenge mainstream curatorial practices and reconnect with objects (Mataga 2018). As museums look beyond their walls and extend their reach to local communities working through objects or sites in the landscape, they are forced to accept that in the production of heritage at local levels, "materiality is not in opposition to spirituality" (Haber 2016 60). As argued by Walklate (2018), in engaging with the world outside their normative, museums accept and acknowledge laughter, embodiment and temporality, shedding their problematic association with heterotopia and allowing ethnographic museums to be recognized as active agents in the socio-political worlds around them.

In such engagements, as the museums look beyond their configuration of being modern knowledge institutions, they challenge their own practices by "departing from Western ontologies, networking with localities and produce a move towards local epistemes" (Haber and Gnecco 2007; Haber 2016: 62). The acknowledgement of local knowledge that has existed at the margins of the processes of knowledge production allows the previously marginalised local communities to enter into the museum and engender new relationships where the non-experts become active participants in curatorial exchanges. As the museums acknowledge the way society deals with the past and its remains, they enter into a dialogue with indigenous communities challenging the asymmetrical relationships entrenched by their previous regimes of engagement.

Case studies at Mutare highlight the importance of deconstructing and challenging the tainted history of museums and skewed knowledge flows that were inculcated through the colonial encounters between European and African museums. Any collaborative programmes between locals and the museums need to acknowledge and embrace the local practices embedded in the specific ways that local communities relate to the past. In the case of southern Africa, these are usually manifest through concepts of sacredness, ritual practices and claims of ancestral ties to objects, landscapes or sites. They are embedded in oral traditions, locally produced histories, rituals and forms of visitation that foreground age-old traditions, which are deliberately altered and reformulated in the present and are considered to be crucial aspects of the local communities' history or culture. Thus, rather than promoting fixed values or emphasising material forms, museums should increasingly incorporate the spiritual and non-material dimensions of the artefacts in their safekeeping. Acknowledging and including locally-derived narratives and practices needs to become the bedrock on which any effective international cooperation can operate (Mataga and Chabata, 2012; Mataga 2018). The museums in Africa, through such a recourse to the local ways of knowing, can perhaps begin to exorcise its history of epistemologies of injustice (Vawda 2019) and misrepresentation, dehumanisation and marginalisation of that which is local and African.

Bibliography

Abungu, G. (2001). Museums: Arenas for Dialogue or Confrontation. *ICOM News* 2: 15–18.

Abungu, G. (2002). Opening Up New Frontiers: Museums of the 21st Century. In P. U. Argren and S. Nyman (eds). *Museums 2000: Confirmation or Challenge*. Stockholm: ICOM Sweden and the Swedish Museum Association, pp. 37–43.

Abungu, G. (2006). Africa and Its Museums: Changing of Pathways? In B. T. Hoffman (ed). *Art and Cultural Heritage: Law, Policy, and Practice*. New York, NY: Cambridge University Press, pp. 386–393.

Abungu, G. (2019). Museums: Geopolitics, Decolonisation, Globalisation and Migration. *Museum International* 71 (281–282–281–282): 62–71.

Abungu, L. (2005). Museums and Communities in Africa: Facing the New Challenges. *Public Archaeology* 4 (2–3–2–3): 151–154.

Bennett, T. (1995). *The Birth of the Museum*: History, Theory, Politics. New York: Routledge.

Bjerregaard, P. (2019). Exhibitions as research, curator as distraction. In: Malene Vest Hansen, Anne Folke Henningsen & Anne Gregersen (eds). *Curatorial Challenges: Interdisciplinary Perspectives on Contemporary Curating.* London: Routledge, pp. 108–120.

Boast, R. (2011). Neocolonial Collaboration: Museum as Contact Zone Revisited. *Museum Anthropology* 34 (1–1): 56–70.

Butler, S. and Lehrer, E. (2016). Introduction: Curatorial Dreaming. In S. R. Butler and E. Lehrer (eds). *Curatorial Dreams*. London: McGill-Queen's University Press, pp. 3–26.

Clifford, J. (2007). The Quai Branly in Process. *October* 120 (3–3): 3–23.

Coombes, A. (2003). *History After Apartheid: Visual Culture and Public Memory in a Democratic South Africa*. Durham, NC: Duke University Press.

Corsane, G. (2004). Transforming Museums and Heritage in Postcolonial and Post-Apartheid South Africa: The Impact of Processes of Policy Formulation and New Legislation Social Analysis. *The International Journal of Anthropology* 48 (1–1): 5–15.

Dahre, U. J. (2019). On the Way Out? The Current Transformation of Ethnographic Museums. In V. Golding and J. Walklate (eds). *Museums and Communities: Diversity, Dialogue and Collaborations in an Age of Migrations*. Cambridge: Cambridge Scholars Publishing, pp. 61–87.

Davison, P. (2005). Museums and the Reshaping of Memory In G. Corsane (ed). *Heritage, Museums and Galleries: An Introductory Reader*. London: Routledge, pp. 184–194.

De Palma, M. (2019). Selfies, Yoga and Hip Hop: Expanding the Roles of Museums. In V. Golding and J. Walklate (eds). *Museums and Communities: Diversity, Dialogue and Collaborations in an Age of Migrations*. Cambridge: Cambridge Scholars Publishing, pp. 230–245.

Golding, V. and Walklate, J. (2019). Introduction. Crossing the Frontier: Locating Museums and Communities in an Age of Migrations. In V. Golding and J. Walklate (eds). Cambridge: Cambridge Scholars Publishing, pp. 1–20.

Haber, A. and Gnecco C. (2007). "Virtual Forum: Archaeology and Decolonization." *Archaeologies: Journal of the World Archaeological Congress* 3 (3): 390–412.

Hooper – Greenhill. E (2007). 'Interpretive communities, strategies and repertoires' In Sheila Watson, S, ed, *Museums and their Communities*. London: Routledge.

Hansen, M. Henningsen, A., and Gregersen, A. (eds). (2019). Introduction. In *Curatorial Challenges: Interdisciplinary Perspectives on Contemporary Curating*. London: Routledge, pp. 1–6.

La Salle, M. J. (2010). Community Collaboration and Other Good Intentions. Archaeologies. *Journal of the World Archaeological Congress* 6 (3–3): 401–422.

Mataga, J. (2018). Museum Objects, Local Communities and Curatorial Shifts in African Museums. In T. Laely, M. Meyer and R. Schwere (eds). *Museum Cooperation between Africa and Europe. A New Field for Museum Studies*. Bielefeld: Transcript and Kampala: Fountain Publishers. pp. 85–97

Mataga, J. and Chabata, F. M. (2012). The Power of Objects: Colonial Museum Collections, Collectors and Changing Contexts. *International Journal of the Inclusive Museum* 4 (2): 81–94.

Onciul, B. (2019). Community Engagement, Indigenous Heritage and the Complex Figure of the Curator: Foe, Facilitator, Friend or Forsaken. In P. Schorch, C. McCarthy and E. Durr (eds). Manchester: Manchester University Press, pp. 159–175.

Pratt, Mary, L.M. L. (1992). Arts of the Contact Zone. *Profession*, 91: 33–40.

Pham, C.T. (2019). "How Museums Identify and Faces Challenges with Diverse Communities." In Viv Golding and Jen Walklate (eds). *Museums and Communities: Diversity, Dialogue and Collaborations in an Age of Migrations*. Cambridge: Cambridge Scholars Publishing. pp.106–119.

Rassool, C. (2006). Community Museums, Memory Politics and Social Transformation in South Africa. In I. Karp, C. A. Kratz, G. Buntinx, L. Swaja and T. Ybarra-Frausto (eds). *Museum Frictions: Public Cultures/Global Transformations*. Durham, NC: Duke University Press, pp. 286–321.

Rassool, C. (2018). Building a Critical Museology in Africa. A Foreword by Ciraj Rassool. In L. Thomas, M. Meyer, and R. Schwere (eds). *Museum Cooperation Between Africa and Europe: A New Field for Museum Studies.* Bielefeld, Germany and Kampala, Uganda: Transcript Verlag and Fountain Publishers. pp. 1–3

Sandahl, J. (2019). The Museum Definition as the Backbone of ICOM. *Museum International* 71 (281–282–281–282): 1–9.

Sandell, R. (2007). *Museums, Prejudice, and the Reframing of Difference.* London: Routledge

Schorch, P., McCarthy, C., and Durr, E. (2019). Introduction: Conceptualising Curatopia. In P. Schorch, C. McCarthy, and E. Durr (eds). *Curatopia, Museums and the Future of Curatorship*. Manchester: Manchester University Press, pp. 1–16.

Shelton, A. 2018. Heterodoxy and the Internationalization and Regionalization of Museums and Museology. In L. Thomas, M. Meyer, and R. Schwere (eds). *Museum Cooperation Between Africa and Europe: A New Field for Museum Studies*. Bielefeld, Germany and Kampala, Uganda: Transcript Verlag and Fountain Publishers, pp. xv–xvi.

Simon, N. (2010). *The Participatory Museum*. Retrieved January 2, 2019 from http://www.participatorymuseum.org/read/

Sweet, J. and Kelly, M. (2019). *Museum Development and Cultural Representation: Developing the Kelabit Highlands Community Museum*. London: Routledge.

Vawda, S. (2019). Museums and the Epistemology of Injustice: From Colonialism to Decoloniality. *Museum International* 71 (281–282): 72–79.

Vilches, F., Christina, G., Ayala, P., and Ulises, C. (2015). The Contemporary Past of San Pedro de Atacama, Northern Chile: Public Archaeology? *Archaeologies* 11 (3): 372–399.

Walklate, J. (2018). Heterotopia or Carnival Site? Rethinking the Ethnographic Museum. *Museum Worlds* 6 (1–1): 32–47.

Index

For Product Safety Concerns and Information please contact our EU representative GPSR@taylorandfrancis.com
Taylor & Francis Verlag GmbH, Kaufingerstraße 24, 80331 München, Germany

www.ingramcontent.com/pod-product-compliance
Lightning Source LLC
LaVergne TN
LVHW010927110826
845149LV00013B/2502

* 9 7 8 1 0 3 2 0 1 9 1 6 1 *